THE
OR
GA
HA

Micha

D0532727

This book should be returned/renewed by the latest date shown above. Overdue items incur charges which prevent self-service renewals. Please contact the library.

Wandsworth Libraries
24 hour Renewal Hotline
www.wandsworth.gov.uk

THE CROWOOD PRESS

LONDON BOROUGH OF WANDSWORTH	
9030 00002 7225 6	
Askews & Holts	02-Aug-2012
635.0484	£16.99
	WWX0009711/0009

First published in 2007 by
The Crowood Press Ltd
Ramsbury, Wiltshire
SN8 2HR

© Michael Littlewood 2007

All rights reserved. No part of this publication may be reproduced or transmitted in any form or by any means, electronic or mechanical, including photocopy, recording, or in any information storage and retrieval system, without the prior written permission of the publishers.

British Library Cataloguing-in-Publication Data
A catalogue record for this book is available from the British Library

ISBN 978 1 86126 936 2

Designed by Andrew Crane

Printed and bound in China
by 1010 Printing International Ltd

The balanced Eco-system —

Nothing happens
in living nature
that is not in relation
to the whole

I HAVE OFTEN THOUGHT that if heaven had given me choice of my position and calling, it would have been on a rich spot of earth, well watered, and near a good market for the production of the garden. No occupation is so delightful to me as the culture of the earth, and no culture comparable to that of the garden. Such a variety of subjects, some one always coming to perfection, the failure of one thing repaired by the success of another, and instead of one harvest a continued one through the year. Under a total want of demand except for our family table, I am still devoted to the garden. But though an old man, I am but a young gardener.

THOMAS JEFFERSON
To Charles Willson Peale, August 20, 1811

Contents

Illustrations

Foreword

The term 'organic gardening' has always been one that never sat entirely comfortably for me. Strictly speaking, the word 'organic' simply means 'of living origin', while a chemist might point out that organic refers to the chemistry of carbon – the building blocks of life. Ironically, carbon-based chemicals include some of the most notorious pollutants of our time, such as DDT and Dioxin, and, indeed, the thousands of tons of noxious gas, soot and ash produced every day by the burning of fossil fuels.

Strangely then, when applied to gardening, the word 'organic' has come to mean the systematic use of techniques that mirror naturally occurring systems. Despite the confusion of terminology, however, whatever you decide to call them, the best and most sustainable systems for horticulture have always been those that attempt to find environmentally friendly ways to cultivate the land, working with, rather than against, nature. Whilst I prefer the term 'environmentally friendly gardening', it lacks a certain catchiness, and the term 'organic gardening' looks set to stay. Call it what you like though, gardening should never be simply a set of techniques, but a whole philosophy of how to get the best from the soil around us.

Origins of the Organic Gardening Movement — From the point of view of gardening, the organic movement can be dated back to the 1940s, when agricultural production and the use of pesticides increased in the years after the Second World War. In many aspects, however, the principles of organic gardening have been practised for centuries. Ancient writers, among them Pliny and Virgil, commented on the importance of 'good husbandry to the health of the land'. Thomas Tusser, in his classic work of 1580 entitled *Five Hundred Points of Good Husbandry*, recommends crop rotation to maintain good health. The classic English garden writer of the 17th century, John Evelyn, begins his *Kalendarium Hortense* with a section describing how to enrich the ground in January with 'horfe and sheeps dung efpecially, that you may have fome of two years preparation'.

Much of the current interest in organic gardening began in the 1960s, with increasing concern about growing levels of environmental damage being caused by pesticides and other agrochemicals. If they were causing so much damage to the world around us, then surely they must ultimately affect us?

The 'organic' approach aims to reduce the effect that our gardens, farms and cities have upon the wider natural environment. Activities such as re-cycling, using sustainably produced materials, and avoiding pesticides and other harmful agrochemicals, all help in this. Organic gardening is often described as being a more natural way to garden. This can make it appear to be somehow revolutionary. In many ways, however, organic gardening could be said to be counter-revolutionary. It aims to avoid artificial inputs and gains. Instead, it draws from a vast resource of wisdom amassed over 10,000 years of experience. Much of the so-called conventional wisdom is in fact very recent and most of our grandparents were naturally 'organic gardeners'. Quite simply, it is the synthesis of good horticultural practice and an awareness of our impact upon our surroundings.

Whilst it is almost impossible to reduce your impact upon the planet entirely – we affect things by simply being here – your aim should always be to aspire to the ideal solution. Almost all of us face compromise on a daily basis and understand that practicalities outweigh personal ideals. With perseverance and practice, however, it is possible to become less compromised in the confines of your own garden. Simple planning and observance of good gardening practice can steadily improve your organic credentials. The more self-sufficient your garden becomes, the more likely it is to be environmentally friendly.

Ultimately, the aim of all gardeners, whether they are landscaping a city garden, tending a country estate or growing home-produced vegetables, is to make choices appropriate to their own situation. It is better to move a few steps towards an environmentally friendly way, then, than to ignore it completely.

Michael Lavelle, Senior Lecturer in
Landscape Management, Writtle College

INTRODUCTION

The Purpose

The main purpose of this book is to provide the organic gardener with basic information for successful organic growing in an easy and quick way for referral. There is nothing more frustrating than trying to remember which gardening book contains the relevant basic information required at a particular stage of gardening. Wherever possible, charts, tables, lists, and so on, are provided, rather than long pages of text.

It is, I hope, the ultimate gardener's *aide-mémoire*.

The book has been divided into seven sections. The first is 'The Basics', which provides data on climate, geology and soils for England and Wales. The second deals with the plants. Knowing all the plant names, especially the botanical ones, is useful, as they can then be placed into the respective families. This in turn helps the gardener to know their needs and requirements much better.

The third section deals with the planning of growing vegetables. It may seem like an unnecessary chore, particularly if the plot is very small, but it is essential if a more successful and satisfactory outcome is to be realized in return for all the gardener's efforts.

'The Ground', in Section Four, is the foundation of the edible garden. Without this there can be no successful organic produce. The soil needs even more care and attention lavished upon it than the plants. Yet how often is the reverse the case with so many gardeners. To be able to feel and smell the soil and know that it is in good heart should be every gardener's duty.

Section Five deals with the actual growing and the various ways in which it can be achieved, along with watering and mulching methods.

Plants may require protection and Section Six provides the many different ways in which this can be undertaken, particularly for the organic gardener who aims to enlist the support of wildlife.

Finally, Section Seven provides a reminder of tasks to be done each month in the edible garden, along with a Glossary, Conversion Tables Bibliography, Acknowledgements and Index.

The Fundamental Ideas

Most people are familiar with the term 'organic gardening', especially if they have anything to do with agriculture or horticulture and the production of safe foodstuffs. The expression is admittedly inexact but everyone knows what it means. Generally speaking, we understand 'organic' to mean a form of gardening that does not rely on poisons to control pests, diseases and weeds and does not use artificial fertilizers; its purpose is to avoid deleterious influences of any sort. Nevertheless, traditional methods of tilling the ground are often still employed. The soil is turned in the usual garden beds and manure is dug into it. What is more, there is often heavy manuring of a specific nature, appropriate only to the needs of the plant population growing in a particular bed in that particular year.

Treatment of this type with mineral fertilizers can disturb the steady rhythm in the life of the soil. In this way, organic gardening, although it does not use poisons, fails to take advantage of all the pure, high-quality nutrients available from natural sources. In view of the danger to which the environment is exposed nowadays, gardeners must surely be asking themselves to what extent they must adopt a positive approach in their work and abandon a negative one. Fortunately, our own researches will supply an answer to this question.

If we are to garden in a way that will be helpful to the environment, we may have to radically re-orientate our activities, whether we are working in the vegetable patch or in the orchard. Not only this, but we should also try to cultivate beautiful and well laid out gardens, full of glorious colours and delicate scents which are a source of strength and joy.

The garden is inhabited by an animal world which can live there in accordance with the laws of nature. All creatures are more or less useful to us when we know their living conditions and take these into account; even the 'pests' are useful as indicators of our omissions or mistakes. These are not the only factors that enter into organic (and trouble-free) gardening and need careful consideration. It is true that the gardener is not a party to the dumping of industrial waste on the environment or to the pollution of air and water, but he should endeavour to utilize all garden and household refuse as far as possible for keeping the land fertile without outside help.

Pests and plant diseases are not just things to be fought with the help of chemicals; they point to faults in cultivation and ought to be regarded in that light. Given the opportunity, the garden itself will achieve a balance between the conflicting interests of its plants and animals, its microflora and microfauna. Chemical control uses up our energy resources and is an unnecessary burden on the environment. By adopting sensible preventive measures of plant protection, the gardener who works organically leaves no polluted water behind him and, thanks to his special mode of cultivation, actually saves water instead of pouring it down the drain.

The buying of garden accessories should be minimal. Simply by utilizing plant growth and energy from the sun, the gardener can prepare soil in which micro-organisms will flourish, this being a prerequisite for the growth of the higher plants. He or she will also seek to promote a healthy cycle between soil and plants by returning everything that grows in the garden to the soil as an active fertilizer assisting future growth. In this way, crops will be assured and yields will be high. Two things are essential: learning to see connections and the absorption of sensible, reliable knowledge.

Acknowledgement: *Companion Planting* by Gertrud Franck
Thorsons Publishing Group

The Guidelines

'These guidelines, my golden rules, evolved over the past seven years as I wrestled with designs for edible gardens that would easily fit into busy lives. Each rule contains a hidden R factor – the Reality coefficient. This factor lumps all of Murphy's Laws into one gigantic mathematical mess. Never underestimate the R factor in your garden, much less in your life.

'As simple as these rules seem, some are consistently ignored. As with all rules, break them only if you are willing to face the consequences. But remember that breaking rules can lead to creative breakthroughs. So be flexible – try to follow the rules, but if you can't, have fun creating your own additions and refinements.'

Robert Kourik

Enjoy your garden – if it's just drudgery, you're doing something wrong. If your garden becomes drudgery, why bother? Do something else instead that is pleasurable. You won't starve. Plan to make it easy to relax, recline and recreate in your edible garden.

You have a lot to do besides gardening – don't let your edible garden take you over. We all have jobs, families, friends and other leisure pastimes. Landscaping is great fun and therapy, but expect to let some areas of the edible garden change or even die. As your life changes, modify your garden to suit it.

Be lazy – let nature work for you. Learn how to use natural, biological processes to your advantage. Nature works 24 hours a day, and there are many ways to co-operate with nature to grow our food.

Turn limitations into virtues. Turn the restraints of your property inside out and make your edible garden pull together as a productive environment. Put plants in the right places to promote their best features.

Seek out the wisdom of your neighbours – someone else might just know more than you do. Most neighbourhoods still have the living heritage of older, lifelong gardeners. They can give more good information about gardening in your locale than any book.

Your edible garden is a community – a whole made up of individuals. The forest doesn't mourn the death of an individual tree. The role of a single plant is to serve the group as a whole. How the pieces, bugs, animals and plants work together is the most important aspect of a healthy edible garden. Respect the pieces, but work toward the betterment of the whole.

Time and money spent early means time and money saved later. An extra buck spent now for a lower-maintenance garden will save you many times that dollar each year for years to come.

Plan in advance – make your mistakes on paper, not in your garden. Paper mistakes are less costly than landscaping mistakes. Sketch out several options and take the time to consider each. Review, re-think, get second opinions, and re-do the plan. It can be costly to be impatient.

Plan for the unexpected – nature will be, in all probability, unpredictable. The climate is getting more, not less, erratic. Plan to have options for several extremes of weather if you do not like to gamble with the food you are growing.

Start ever so small. A 100-square-foot vegetable bed is the largest area for a new gardener. Make this tiny plot picture perfect, then add on another 100 square feet each year until the Peter Principle is activated. That is, increase the area of the vegetable beds just short of the point where you can no longer master them.

Learn the multiple uses of plants to double the benefits of your garden without doubling size or work. Many plants can serve more than one function. Some cool the house in the summer while ripening tasty fruits or nuts. Others have nutritious roots and leaves. Others kill pests and are edible. When possible, choose those plants that have multiple benefits.

Plant your vegetables no farther from the kitchen than you can throw the kitchen sink. There is a correlation between the distance to the kitchen and the demise of a vegetable bed. Almost literally, for every foot farther from the kitchen sink the vegetables get forgotten a week sooner. The most distant vegetable beds return to weeds the soonest.

Acknowledgement: *Designing and Maintaining Your Edible Landscape Naturally.* Robert Kourik, Metamorphic Press USA

1 THE BASICS

- Climate
- Soils

CLIMATE

Gardeners, like farmers, need to have information about the climate, the geology, the soils, the hydrology (water) and the ecology of their country, their region, their locality and finally their own property. Armed with this information, you can then use it to your own advantage for the more successful growing of edible plants by using various methods for amelioration. For example, by the protection from strong and prevailing winds on an exposed site; improving soils which are low in fertility; or ensuring that rainfall does not cause the ground to become waterlogged.

Knowing the ecology of your own locality and region helps you to understand the advantages and disadvantages of your own site. It will help you to garden in harmony with nature. The past will always offer clues which can be found helpful in the present use of the land.

Through the internet, there is now available considerable information such as the climate from the Meteorological Office and soils from the National Soils Resources Institute.

Guide to Seasons

	Southern UK 50°- 53°N	*Northern UK 53°N+*
Early spring	March	April
Mid-spring	April	May
Late spring	May	May-June
Early summer	June	June-July
Mid-summer	July	July
Late summer	August	August
Early autumn	September	August-Sept.
Mid-autumn	October	October
Late autumn	November	November
Early winter	December	December
Mid-winter	January	January
Late winter	February	February-Mar.

Phenological Map

Phenology is a study which relates climate to the development of plant life; for example, the times at which a plant starts to grow, or matures. As isotherms on maps connect places experiencing the same temperatures, so isophenes connect places where the same stage in plant development is taking place. The phenological map shows the dates on which grass begins to grow in various parts of Britain – this is, generally speaking, when the temperature reaches 6°C (42°F). The minimum temperature for growth (called the 'zero temperature') of a plant varies from species to species. For peas, for example, the zero temperature is 4°C (40°F), for potatoes, 7°C (45°F) and, for sweetcorn, 10°C (50°F).

Superimposed on the map are the isotherms for July, 15°C (59°F), running east-west, and January, 5°C (41°F), running north-south. They indicate the basic regional differences in the British climate. The dry northeast has cool summers and cold winters. The rainy northwest has cool summers and mild winters. The dry southeast has warm summers and cool winters. The rainy southwest has warm summers and mild winters.

The temperature map right, extends the July and January isotherms from Britain over Europe to indicate the general weather pattern there.

In January the temperature increases as you travel westwards from the 5°C (41°F) isotherm, while in July it increases southwards from the 15°C (59°F) isotherm. Grass begins to grow when the temperature reaches 6°C (42°F), and this indicates the start of the general planting season. The map shows that growth in the southwest can be a fortnight or more earlier than in the northeast.

Climate — By Region

South-west Scotland and Northern Ireland
The growing period is long; near the coast the average frost-free period can be some 225 days. Summers are generally cool with cloudy skies. Rainfall averages are high enough for wet years to be problematic. Some of the best strawberries and potatoes come from Auchincruive on the Ayrshire coast

North-west England and North Wales
Slow southward improvement begins to affect garden climates. Wind speeds are less, though north-westerly gales may persist. Summers are rarely hot, but the growing season is long; late frosts occur inland. In lowland areas, summer rainfall is near the optimum and here are successful market gardening areas. In the hills rain is excessive.

Southern Ireland
Frosts are rare compared with England, rainfall is adequate and the temperature range is reasonable, especially in the winter. Sunshine is generally deficient, being highest in the south-east. Grey skies predominate and may be responsible for discouraging potential gardeners. High humidity can encourage plant diseases.

North-west Scotland
Proximity to the Atlantic gives an early start to growth and late frosts are absent on the coasts. Summers are cool, sunshine amounts on the low side. Rainfall is in excess of plant needs. Sheltered sites provide isolated examples of gardening skill, as at Inverewe; elsewhere shelter, natural or contrived and preferably both, is essential.

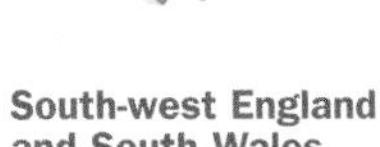

South-west England and South Wales
The earliest springs and latest autumns occur here. There is a long growing period with less frost risk than anywhere else, especially on the coast. Rainfall is higher than in the east and summer temperatures are slightly lower. The garden climate is good, except for strong winds and salt damage.

Channel Islands
The sunniest and warmest part in the British Isles with a 365 day growing season. The main disadvantage is lack of summer rainfall; with supplies stretched to the utmost by the influx of summer visitors, watering can cause problems. Winter gales are common, but summer winds are usually less violent.

North-east Scotland
Winds from the north and east are strong and cold. Springs are late, with a high frost risk and autumn is early. Sunshine hours are few, although occasional day temperatures can be high with southerly winds. Rainfall is less excessive than in the west and some sheltered areas around Inverness and in the eastern glens offer reasonable garden climates.

South-east Scotland
Conditions slowly improve. Springs are still late, with danger of late frosts, but sunshine totals and warmth increase and temperatures are higher. North and east winds predominate and southern aspects are most favourable. Rainfall averages decrease and droughts may be a problem in the Lothians.

North-east England
The growing season is late, with dates ranging from early April in South Yorkshire to late April in Northumberland. Summers are still on the cool side, but the Pennines give some protection from westerly winds. Sunshine totals are low except on the coast; rainfall averages decrease in Humberside and the old East Riding.

South-east England
With some justification, Kent is called the 'Garden of England'. Spring is late, especially after a cold winter, but growth persists toward the end of the year. Sunshine averages are good, rainfalls though below the optimum, are higher than in East Anglia. Summer temperatures are usually high.

Midland England
The growing season is of some 240-260 days; danger of late frosts is appreciable, due to distance from the sea; sunshine hours are fewer than in coastal areas. Conditions are fairly good with a reasonable chance of warm summers. Rainfall is slightly lower than the optimum; the East Midlands are liable to spring droughts. Winds are generally lighter than in most other areas.

East Anglia
The main gardening disadvantage is the low rainfall. Another difficulty is the liability to wind erosion in a dry spring, shelter being almost non-existent. The growing season is long, but with danger of late frosts. Summer temperatures are generally high, except with easterly winds. Winters can be severe.

From *Which - Kind of Garden*
By kind permission of the Consumers Association

Frosts

There is a difference between an air frost – when the temperature of the air itself drops below freezing – and a ground frost, which is not so cold, with only the surface of the ground being affected where the dew freezes. This happens because cold air falls at night and accumulates at low points at ground level. Since the air is not freezing, foliage is not affected. Many tender plants can resist a ground frost, but will be affected by an air frost. Even very tender plants need only modest protection from ground frost.

Spring frosts

Below is a rough guide to the last time an air frost is most likely to occur (ground frosts might be later) in different parts of the UK:

Plymouth Bristol	mid-April mid-April	Southwest
Cardiff	late April	South Wales
London	early May	Southeast
Cambridge	early May	East
Birmingham	late May	Midlands & Mid-Wales
Liverpool	early April	Northwest & North Wales
Leeds	early May	Northeast
Edinburgh Isle of Skye Wick	early May early April late May	Scotland

A number of other factors need to be taken into account —

- distance from the sea and height above sea level
- late frost occurs further inland
- spring takes longer to reach higher ground – approximately two days for every 30m rise in height
- dry, light soil freezes more readily than damp soil and is therefore a risk for longer
- frost pockets can form in odd places. Cold air flows downhill like water into valleys or dips in the ground, and a valley can have more frost than a hillside above it
- to minimize the risk of a late frost, garden on low ground (but without any frost pockets) on the southwest coast with naturally damp soil.

Frost pockets

If a part of the garden is vulnerable to 'collecting' frost, move a barrier out of the way to allow the cold air to flow through and escape. Simply replacing a solid fence with an open trellis can eliminate a frost pocket.

Autumn frosts

The first widespread frosts in the central UK usually happen in October, although, closer to the coast, the first frost is likely to occur later. The extreme western edges often escape frost until November. The first extensive frosts are often, although not 100 per cent reliably, preceded by north to northwesterly winds.

The pattern of arrival of autumn is much the same as for spring in reverse, so the last places to get frosts are the southwest and areas near the coast. Again, high ground will tend to see frosts earlier than lower-lying land.

Plymouth Bristol	late Oct late Oct	Southwest
Cardiff	late Oct	South Wales
London	early Oct	Southeast
Cambridge	early Oct	East
Birmingham	late Sept	Midlands & Mid-Wales
Liverpool	late Oct	Northwest & North Wales
Leeds	late Sept	Northeast
Edinburgh Isle of Skye Wick	late Sept early Nov early Oct	Scotland

Typical garden and its Microclimates

Even a small garden can contain a wide variety of microclimates, ranging from cool, shady corners, to hot, dry areas. A proper assessment of the growing conditions that prevail in your garden allows you to choose the right plants for the right place.

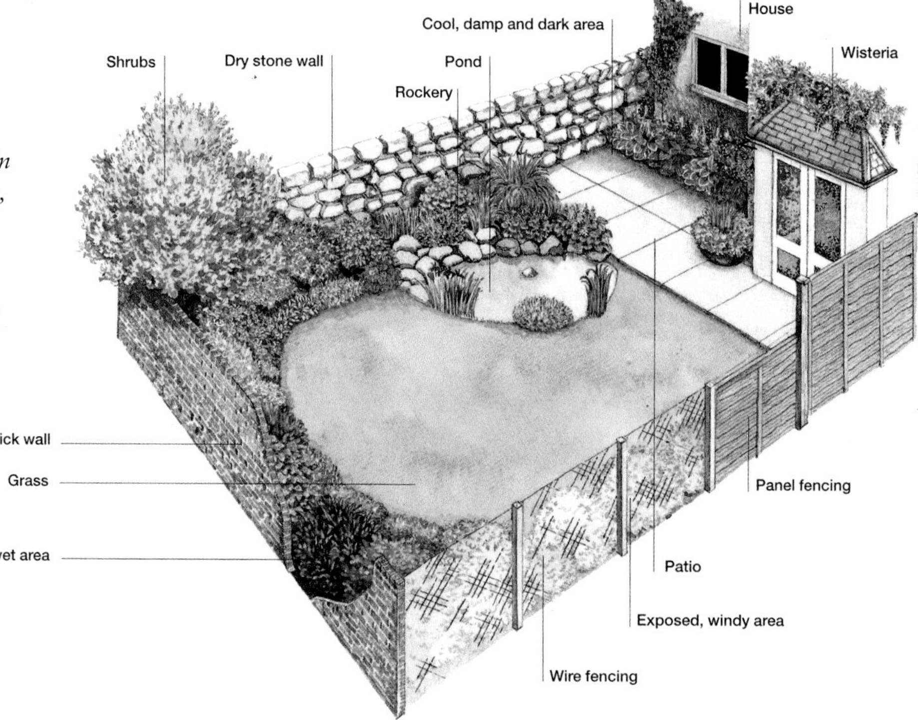

SOILS

Soilscapes* of England & Wales

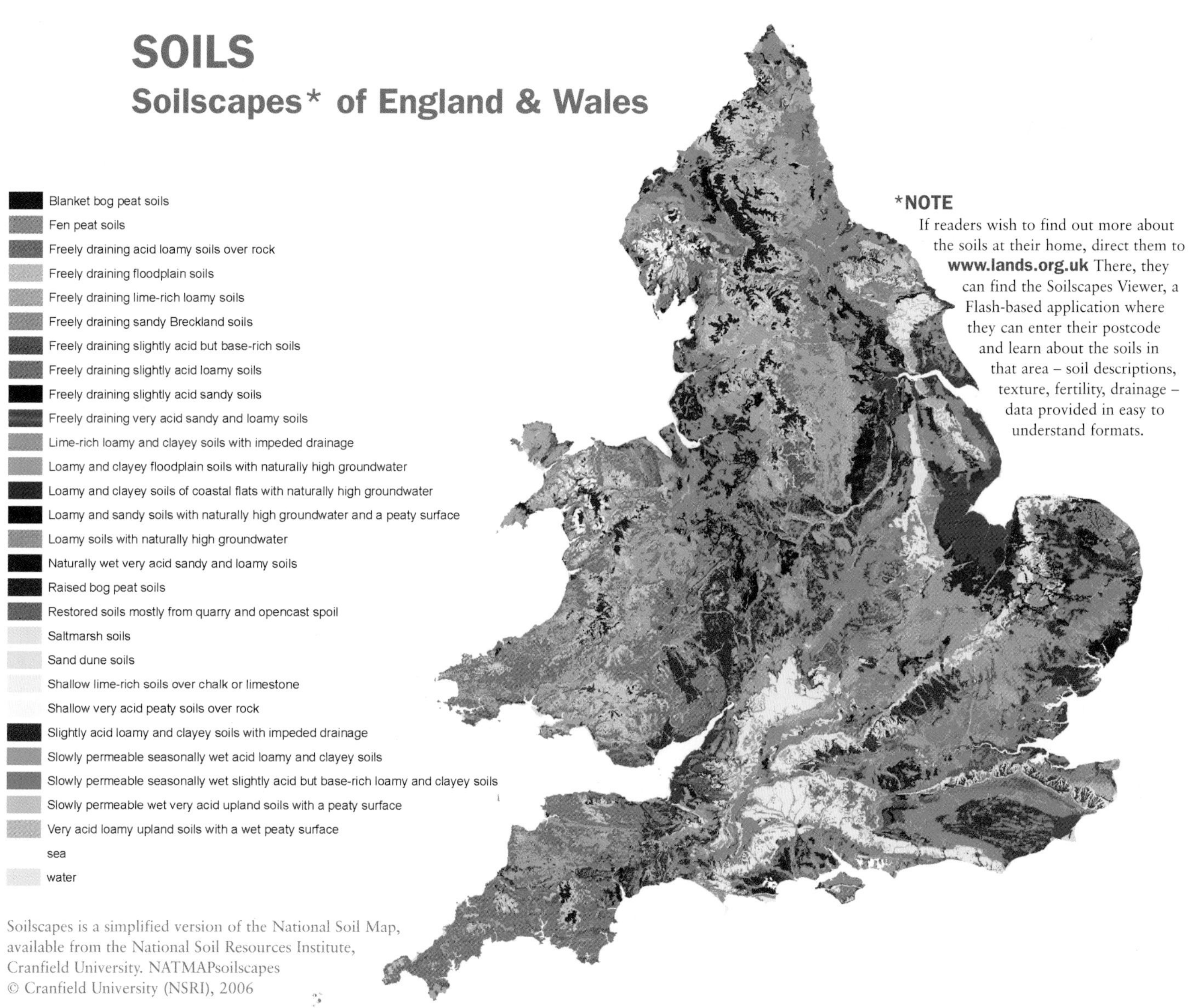

***NOTE**

If readers wish to find out more about the soils at their home, direct them to **www.lands.org.uk** There, they can find the Soilscapes Viewer, a Flash-based application where they can enter their postcode and learn about the soils in that area – soil descriptions, texture, fertility, drainage – data provided in easy to understand formats.

Soilscapes is a simplified version of the National Soil Map, available from the National Soil Resources Institute, Cranfield University. NATMAPsoilscapes
© Cranfield University (NSRI), 2006

LETTUCE
MIX

2 THE PLANTS

- Natural Orders and Their Families
- Botanical Names

NATURAL ORDERS AND THEIR FAMILIES

THE ORDER

Vegetables are arranged in families in a traditional botanical order and the vegetables are listed alphabetically with their respective family.

Plant Name	*Family*	*Plant Name*	*Family*	*Plant Name*	*Family*
Artichoke Chinese	*Lamiaceae*	Chicory	*Asteraceae*	Peas	*Papilionaceae*
Artichoke Globe	*Asteraceae*	Chives	*Liliaceae*	Pepper, green	*Solanaceae*
Artichoke Jerusalem	*Asteraceae*	Courgette	*Cucurbitaceae*	Potato	*Solanaceae*
Asparagus	*Liliaceae*	Cucumber	*Cucurbitaceae*	Pumpkin	*Cucurbitaceae*
Asparagus pea	*Papilionaceae*	Endive	*Asteraceae*	Radish	*Brassicaceae*
Aubergine	*Solanaceae*	Fennel florence	*Apiaceae*	Salsify	*Asteraceae*
Bean, broad	*Papilionaceae*	Garlic	*Liliaceae*	Scorzonera	*Asteraceae*
Bean, French (bush)	*Papilionaceae*	Kale	*Brassicaceae*	Seakale	
Bean, pole	*Papilionaceae*	Kohlrabi	*Brassicaceae*	Shallot	*Liliaceae*
Bean, runner	*Papilionaceae*	Lamb's Lettuce	*Valerianaceae*	Spinach	*Chenopodiaceae*
Beetroot	*Chenopodiaceae*	Leek	*Liliaceae*	Spinach (NZ)	*Aizoaceae*
Broccoli	*Brassicaceae*	Lettuce	*Asteraceae*	Squash	*Cucurbitaceae*
Brussels sprouts	*Brassicaceae*	Marrow	*Cucurbitaceae*	Swede	*Brassicaceae*
Cabbage	*Brassicaceae*	Miner's Lettuce	*Portulaceae*	Sweetcorn	*Poaceae*
Carrots	*Apiaceae*	Okra	*Malvaceae*	Swiss chard	*Chenopodiaceae*
Cauliflower	*Brassicaceae*	Onions	*Liliaceae*	Tomato	*Solanaceae*
Celeriac	*Apiaceae*	Parsley	*Apiaceae*	Turnip	*Apiaceae*
Celery	*Apiaceae*	Parsnip	*Apiaceae*		

THE FAMILIES

Knowing which vegetables are related allows gardeners to predict which pests and diseases are likely to affect the plants, whether they should add fertility or not and where the plants should be grown in the plot rotation.

It is often the case that members of a family exploit similar ecological niches and therefore have similar cultural needs. The more related information is to natural conditions, the more sense it makes for the 'edible gardener' to learn about botanical families. The plant families from which vegetables have been developed are listed below in alphabetical order.

FAMILY	Plant
AIZOACEAE	
	NZ Spinach
CHENOPODIACEAE	
	Beetroot
	Good King Henry
	Orache
	Spinach
	Spinach Beet
	Swiss Chard
	Sugar Beet
ASTERACEAE	
	Artichoke – Globe
	Artichoke – Jerusalem
	Cardoon
	Chicory
	Dandelion
	Endive
	Lettuce
	Salsify
	Scorzonera
	Shungiku
	Sunflower

FAMILY	Plant
BRASSICACEAE	
	Broccoli
	Brussels Sprouts
	Cabbage
	Calabrese
	Cauliflower
	Chihli
	Collard
	Cress
	Horseradish
	Kale
	Kohlrabi
	Landcress
	Mizuna
	Mustard
	Pak-choi/Chinese cabbage
	Radish
	Rape
	Rocket
	Seakale
	Swede
	Turnip
	Watercress

FAMILY	Plant
CUCURBITACEAE	
	Bitter gourd
	Chayote
	Courgette
	Cucumber
	Marrow
	Melon
	Pumpkin
	Squash – summer/winter
	Watermelon
POACEAE	
	Barley
	Maize
	Millet
	Oats
	Rice
	Rye
	Sorghum
	Wheat
	Wild Rice

Continued over

FAMILY	Plant
LAMIACEAE	
	Artichoke – Chinese
PAPILIONACEAE	
	Asparagus pea
	Beans - Black
	- Broad
	- Butter
	- French
	- Haricot
	- Jack
	- Pea
	- Runner
	Black gram
	Chickpea
	Green gram
	Lentils
	Liquorice
	Peanut
	Peas
	Pigeon pea
	Soybean

FAMILY	Plant
LILIACEAE	
	Asparagus
	Chives
	Garlic
	Leek
	Onion
	Shallot
	Welsh onion
POLYGONACEAE	
	Rhubarb
PORTULACEAE	
	Miner's Lettuce
SOLANACEAE	
	Aubergine
	Cape gooseberry
	Chilli
	Huckleberry
	Pepper (Capsicums)
	Potato
	Tomato
	Tree tomato

FAMILY	Plant
APIACEAE	
	Carrot
	Celeriac
	Celery
	Fennel
	Lovage
	Parsley
	Parsnip
VALERIANACEAE	
	Lamb's Lettuce

BOTANICAL NAMES

Knowing the botanical names of plants ensures that there are no misunderstandings, as common names vary not only from country to country throughout the world, but even from region to region within the United Kingdom.

VEGETABLES

Common Name	*Botanical Name*
Artichoke Chinese	*Stachys affinis*
Artichoke Globe	*Cyara scolyus*
Artichoke Jerusalem	*Helianthus tuberosas*
Asparagus	*Asparagus officinalis*
Asparagus pea	*Tetragonolobus*
Aubergine	*Purpureus*
Bean, broad	*Solanum melongena*
Bean, French (bush)	*Vicia faba*
Bean, pole	*Phasiolus vulgaris*
Bean, runner	*Phaseolus vulgaris*
Beetroot	*Phaseolus cossineaus*
Broccoli	*Beta vulgaris*
Brussels sprouts	*Brassica oleracea* var. italica
Cabbage	*Brassica oleracea* var. gemmiferra
Carrots	*Brassica oleracea* var. capitata
Cauliflower	*Damens carota* var. sativa
Celeriac	*Brassica oleracea* var. botrytis
Celery	*Apiam grareolens*
Chicory	*Cichorium intybus*
Chives	*Allium schoenoprassum*
Courgette	*Cucurbita pepo*
Cucumber	*Cucumis sativus*
Endive	*Cichorium endivia*
Fennel Florence	*Foenicuulum vulgare* var. azoricum
Garlic	*Allium sativum*

Common Name	*Botanical Name*
Kale	*Brassica oleracea* var. acephala
Kohlrabi	*Brassica caulorapa*
Leek	*Allium porrum*
Lettuce	*Latuca sativa*
Marrow	*Cucurbita pepo*
Onions	*Allium cepa*
Parsley	*Petroselinum crispum*
Parsnip	*Pastinaca sativa*
Peas	*Pisum sativum* var. arrense
Pepper, green	*Capsicum frutessens*
Potato	*Solanum tuberosum*
Pumpkin	*Cucurbita pepo, moschata*
Radish	*Raphanus sativas*
Salsify	*Tragopogon porrifolius*
Scorzonera	*Scorzonera hispanica*
Seakale	*Crambe maritina*
Shallot	*Allium escalonicum*
Spinach	*Spinacia oleracea*
Spinach	*Tetragonia tetragonoides*
Squash	*Cucurbita maxima*
Swede	*Brassica napus*
Sweetcorn	*Zea mays* var. Saccharata
Swiss chard	*Beta vulgaris*
Tomato	*Lycopersicon esculentum*
Turnip	*Brassica napa*

VEGETABLES Chinensis Group

Common Name	*Botanical Name*
Pak choi	*Brassica rapa*
Mizuna greens	*Brassica rapa* var. nipposinica
Chinese cabbage	*Brassica rapa* var. pekinensis
Chilli peppers	*Capsicum spp.*
Curled endive	*Cichorium endiva*
Red chicory	*Cichorium intybus*
Sugar loaf chicory	*Cichorium intybus*

SALAD PLANTS

Common Name	*Botanical Name*
Claytonia/winter purslane	*Monita perfoliata*
Corn salad/lamb's lettuce	*Valerianella locusta*
Cress/garden cress	*Lepidium sativum*
Dandelion	*Taraxacum officinale*
Iceplant	*Mesembryanthemum crystallinum*
Land cress/American land cress	*Barbarea verna*
Leaf radish	*Raphanus sativus*
Mustard	*Sinapsis alba*
Rocket/Mediterranean rocket/ Italian cress/ rucola	*Eruca sativa*
Sorrel	*Rumex*
Summer purslane	*Portulaca oleracea*

HERBS

Common Name	*Botanical Name*
Angelica	*Angelica archangelica*
Anise	*Pimpinella anisum*
Balm Lemon	*Melissa officinalis*
Basil	*Ocimum bassillicum*
Bergamot	*Monarda didyma*
Borage	*Borago officinalis*
Burnet	*Sanguisorba minor*
Caraway	*Carum carvi*
Chamomile (Tea)	*Matricaria recutita*
Chervil	*Anthriscus cerefolium*
Chives	*Allium schoenoprasum*
Clary	*Salvia sclarea*
Coriander	*Coriandrum sativum*
Cumin	*Cuminum cyminum*
Dandelion	*Taraxacum officinale*
Dill	*Anethum graveolens*
Evening Primrose	*Taraxacum officinale*
Fennel – Bronze	*Foeniculum vulgare 'Purpureum'*
Fennel – Common	*Foeniculum vulgare*
Feverfew	*Tanacetum parthenium*
Garlic Chives	*Allium tuberosum*
Garlic Mustard	*Alliara petiolata*
Good King Henry	*Chenopodium bonus-henricus*
Hyssop	*Hyssopus officinale*
Lavender	*Lavandula species*
Lovage	*Levisticum officinale*
Marjoram, Pot	*Origanum onites*
Marjoram, Sweet	*Origanum majorana*
Pennyroyal	*Mentha pulegium*
Peppermint	*Mentha piperita*

HERBS continued

Common Name	*Botanical Name*
Purslane – (Winter & Summer)	*Portulaca oleracea*
Rosemary	*Rosmarinus officinalis*
Sage	*Salvia officinalis*
Savory – Summer	*Satureja hortensis*
Savory – Winter	*Satureja montana*
Soapwort	*Saponaria officinalis*
Sorrel – French	*Rumex scutatus*
Spearmint	*Mentha spicata*
Sweet Cicely	*Myrrhis dorata*
Tansy	*Tanacetum vulgaris*
Tarragon	*Artemisia dracunculoides*
Thyme	*Thymus vulgaris*
Valerian	*Valerian officinalis*
Welsh Onion	*Allium fistulosum*
Wormwood	*Artemisia absinthium*

FRUIT

Common Name	*Botanical Name*
PIP	
Apple	*Malus domestica*
Apple Crab/Cider	*Malus pumila*
Pear	*Pyrus communis*
Quince	*Cydonia vulgaris*
Plum	*Prunus domestica*
Greengages	*Prunus italica*
Apricots	*Prunus armeniaca*
Peaches & Nectarines	*Prunus persica*
Cherry Sweet	*Prunus avium*
Cherry Morello	*Prunus cerasus*

FRUIT continued

Common Name	*Botanical Name*
SOFT	
Mulberry	*Morus nigra and alba*
Fig	*Ficus carica*
Rhubarb	*Rheum rhaponticum*
Strawberry Wild/Alpine	*Fragaria vesca semperflorens*
Blueberry/Bilberry	*Vaccinium species*
Cranberry	*Vaccinium*
Currant, Red/White	*Ribes sativum*
Gooseberry	*Ribes grossularia*
Currant, Black	*Ribes nigrum*
Chokeberry	*Aronia melanocarpa*
Raspberry	*Rubus idaeas*
Blackberry	*Rubus fruiticosus*
Loganberry	*Rubus*
Grape	*Vitis vinefera*
Gooseberry Cape	*Physalis species*
Melon	*Cucumis melo*
Cucumber	*Cucumis satvus*
Water Melon	*Citrullus lanatus*
Orange/Lemon	*Citrus species*
Olive	*Olea europaea*
Gooseberry, Chinese	*Actinidia chinensis*
Passion Fruit	*Passiflora species*
Loquat/Japanese Medlar	*Photinia japonica*
Juneberry	*Amelanchier canadensis*
Myrtle	*Myrtus communis*
Barberry	*Berberis vulgaris*
Medlar	*Mespilus germanica*
Elderberry	*Sambucus nigra*
Juniper berry	*Juniperus communis*

NUTS

Common Name	*Botanical Name*
Almond	*Prunus dulcis*
Pecan Hickory	*Cary species*
Walnut	*Juglans species*
Hazel/Cob/Filbert	*Corylus species*
Chestnut Sweet	*Castania sativa*
Pistachio	*Pistacia vera*
Cashew	*Anacardium occidentale*
Macadamia	*Macadamia ternifolia*
Brazil	*Bertholletia excelsa*
Coconut	*Cocos nucifera*

EDIBLE FLOWERS Ornamental

Common Name	*Botanical Name*
Calendula	*Calendula officinalis*
Carnation	*Dianthus*
Daisy	*Bellis perennis*
Elderflower	*Sambucus nigra*
Nasturtium	*Tropaolum majus*
Rose	*Rosa species*
Sunflower	*Helianthus*
Heartsease/Wild Pansy	*Viola tricolour*
Viola	*Viola odorata*
Lavender	*Lavandula species*
Rosemary	*Rosemarinus officinalis*
Thyme	*Thymus vulgaris*

GRAINS

Common Name	*Botanical Name*
Amaranth	*Amaranthus giganticus*
Barley	*Hordeum distichon*
Oats	*Avena sativa*
Rye	*Secale cereale*
Wheat	*Triticum aestivum*

GREEN MANURE/COVER CROPS

Common Name	*Botanical Name*
Alfalfa (Lucerne)	*Medicago sativa*
Buckwheat	*Fagopytum esculentum*
Clovers – Asilke	*Trifolium hybridum*
Clovers – Crimson	*Trifolium incarnatum*
Clovers – Red	*Trifolium pratense*
Clovers – White	*Trifolium alba*
Bitter Lupin	*Lupinus angustifolius*
Fenugreek	*Trigonella foerumgraecum*
Beans, Field, Fara, Broad	*Vicia faba*
Grazing Rye	*Secale cereale*
Italian Ryegrass	*Lolium species 'Westerwolds'*
Mustard	*Sinapsis alba*
Phacelia	*Phacelia tanacetifolia*
Trefoil	*Medecago lupulina*
Winter Tares/ common vetch	*Vicia sativa*

EDIBLE AQUATIC PLANTS

Common Name	*Botanical Name*	Edible part
Sweet Flag	*Acorus calamas*	Rhizome
Cape Pondweed	*Aponogeton distachyos*	Tubers, seeds
	Beckmannia eruciformis	Tubers, seeds
Flowering Rush	*Butomus umbellatus*	Tubers, seeds
Golden Saxifrages	*Chrysoplenium alternifolium and C. oppositifolium*	Leaves
Creeping Dogwood	*Cornus Canadensis*	Fruit
Galingale	*Cyperus longus*	Roots
Float Grass	*Glyceria fluitans*	Seeds
Gunnera	*Gunnera tinctoria*	Leaf stalks
Watercress	*Nasturtium officinale*	Leaves, seeds
Yellow Water Lily	*Nuphar lutea*	Roots
White Water Lily	*Nymphaea alba*	Leaves, flowers
White Arrow Arum	*Peltandra alba*	Rhizome – cooked. Poisonous raw
Green Arrow Arum	*P. virginica*	
Common Reed	*Phragmites communis*	Roots, seeds
Pickerel Weed	*Pontederia cordata*	Seeds, leaf stalks
Arrow Head	*Sagittaria sagittifolia*	Tubers
Brookweed	*Samolus valerandi*	Leaves
Bulrush	*Scirpus lacustris*	Roots, shoots
Bur-Reed	*Sparganium erectum*	Tubers
Water Chestnut	*Trapa natans*	Seeds
Smaller Reed Mace	*Typha angustifolia*	Rhizome, young shoots, seeds, pollen, young spikes
Greater Reed Mace	*T. latifolia*	
Small Cranberry	*Vaccinium palustre*	Fruit, leaves
Wild Rice	*Zizania acquatica*	Rhizomes, young shoots, stem bases, seeds

A Note on Botanical Names

While common names are widely used, one plant may have several common names, or in different parts of the world a common name may refer to different plants. The system of botanical names used today is known as the Binomial System, devised by the 18th-century Swedish botanist Carl Linnaeus (1707–78). In this system, each plant is classified by using two words in Latin form. The first word is the name of the genus (for example, Thymus) and the second the specific epithet (for example, *vulgaris*); together they provide a universally known name, such as Thymus *vulgaris*.

The Linnaean system of plant classification has been developed so that the entire plant kingdom is divided into a multi-branched family tree according to each plant's botanical characteristics. Plants are gathered into particular families according to the structure of their flowers, fruits or seeds. A family may contain one genus or many. The Asteraceae family, for example, contains over 800 genera, included *Achillea, Arnica* and *Artemisia*, to name but a few, and over 13,000 species.

Plants are cultivated for the garden from the wild to improve their leaf or their flower or their root. This can be done either by selection from seedlings or by spotting a mutation. Such plants are known as 'cultivars' (a term derived from 'cultivated varieties'). Propagation from these varieties is normally done by cuttings or division. Cultivars are given vernacular names, which are shown within quotes – for example, *Thymus* 'Doone Valley' – to distinguish them from wild varieties in Latin form appearing in italics (*Thymus pulegioides*). Sexual crosses between species, usually of the same genus, are known as hybrids and are indicated by a multiplication sign – *Thymus* × *citriodorus*.

Finally, a problem that seems to be getting worse is that plants are undergoing reclassification and long-established names are being changed. This is the result of scientific studies and research whereby it is found either that a plant has been incorrectly identified or that its classification has changed. This book uses the latest information available. Where there has been a recent change in the botanical names, this is shown in brackets.

Acknowledgement: Jekka McVicar,
The Complete Book of Vegetables, Herbs and Fruit

3 THE PLANNING

- Requirements
- Plot Layouts
- Yield Chart
- Vegetable Planning Chart
- Crop Rotation
- Cropping Plans

REQUIREMENTS

The success of any project comes down to detailed planning and there are many examples of those that have, or have not, been successful. Edible gardening is no exception to this rule. Although the task of planning may seem irksome it will always pay dividends.

Checklist

It is essential to know your requirements for the land you have set aside for the growing of vegetables and/or fruit. Completing a checklist is a helpful way to start and an example is as follows:

How much food is to be grown?
How many people are to be fed?
How much time can be devoted to growing edibles?
Is it to be vegetables only?
Will it include perennial plants as well as annuals?
Is it to be vegetables and fruit?
What type of fruit will be grown – soft and/or hard; bush and/or tree?
How much space/land is available?
How much land will be required to meet your requirements?

PLOT LAYOUTS

Once you have decided on the above you can then proceed with selecting the most appropriate layout and system.

Traditional System

This consists of an extensive plot or series of plots in which vegetables can be grown in long, widely spaced rows with adequate space between the rows. The whole area is cultivated and walked on during the process of working the soil, sowing, planting, caring and harvesting.

Advantage

- The whole area is cultivated and manured quickly and easily

Disadvantages

- The soil is walked upon
- The ground becomes compacted
- Not suitable for smaller plots
- Better for use with machinery, ie tractor beds

Bed System

The vegetable garden is divided into narrow plots or beds that are usually separated by paths of wheelbarrow width. Plants are grown at equidistant spacings across the beds.

The beds are usually 2.4 × 1.2m (8 × 4ft), although they can be longer and wider, for example, 3.0 × 1.5m (10 × 5ft).

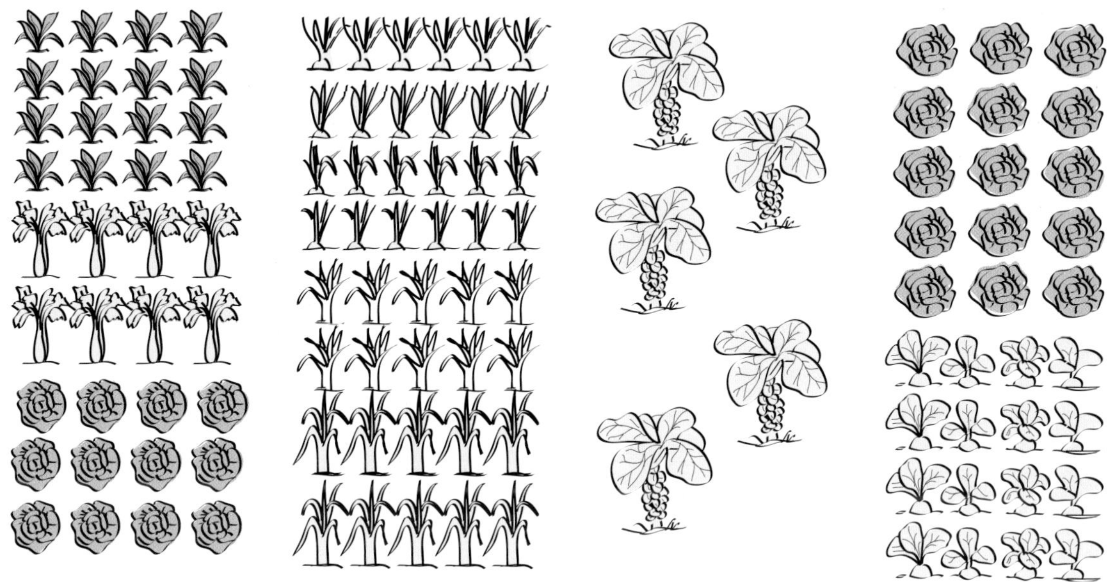

Typical Bed System for Vegetable Crops

A convenient width for vegetable beds is about 1.2m (4ft), with paths 30-40cm (1-1.5ft) wide. To minimize shading from tall plants, orientate them so that their length runs north to south. Plant the crops in blocks rather than rows to give a higher yield.

The beds can be raised if the soil or the drainage is poor or if a better level for working is found to be helpful. Ground-level beds will, in the course of time, become raised by the constant addition of compost and manure.

Advantages

- Allows the work to be done from the paths
- Eliminates the need to walk on the soil
- Protects the soil structure
- Manure and compost is applied to specific growing areas
- Beds become more fertile due to concentration of compost and manure
- Energy is saved by only working the growing beds
- Crop rotation is easier to practise as narrow beds offer more flexibility
- Easier to cover for protection

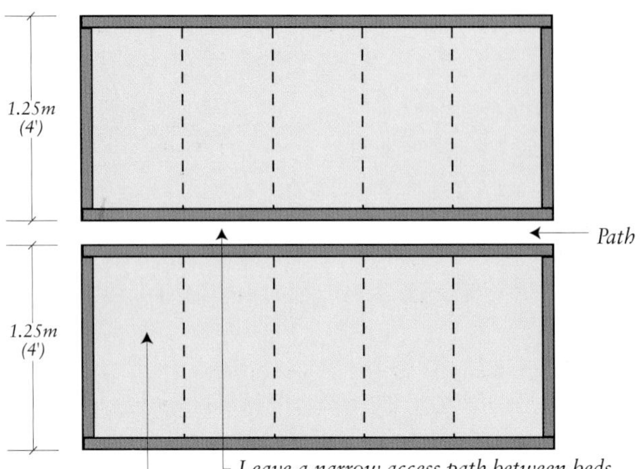

Deep Bed Dimensions

The beds can be as long as is convenient. A 3x1.5m (10x4ft) bed gives a 4.5 sqmetre (40sq.ft) planting area which should produce up to 4 times the yield of a conventional bed of the same size.

A Conventional Bed

The comparatively shallow and compacted layer of topsoil means that roots cannot penetrate deeply and have to be planted further apart. Root crops may be distorted and smaller resulting in lower yields.

A Deep Bed

A deep layer of loose, organically enriched soil encourages roots to penetrate downwards, rather than spreading sideways. This allows the crops to be planted much closer together, resulting in considerably increased yields

Disadvantages

- More room is required overall
- Far more care and attention is required
- Paths need to be kept clean and clear of weeds and debris

Random System

Where space is restricted, vegetables can be grown among ornamental plants in borders using specially selected species to provide colour form and shape.

Advantage

- The whole garden could become one entity provided it is designed accordingly

Disadvantage

- This layout will not result in sufficient crops to feed a family

Potager System

The French traditional layout of plants being grown in formal beds of a special design resulting in a visually pleasing display.

Advantages

- The design of the beds can follow the crop rotation system
- An attractive garden can be created
- Ideal for small spaces

Disadvantages

- Time-consuming
- More energy required

Crop Continuity

To ensure a constant supply of fresh vegetables, it is necessary to produce a scheme for each bed in the overall rotation plan, which, given the vagaries of the weather and inconsistencies in the growth of crops, should be made flexible.

- Decide on the major vegetables you wish to grow
- Indicate on the plan how long the vegetables are to be in the ground
- Follow or proceed them with another major crop
- Where this is impossible, fit short-term and minor vegetables in before or after the main crops or grow a green manure

VEGETABLES FOR THE 'HUNGRY GAP' (late winter/early spring)

Brussels sprouts
Chard
Kale
Leaf beet
Leeks
Parsley
Radish and radish pods
Seedling salads
Sprouting broccoli
Winter cabbage
Winter cauliflower
Winter spinach

Also take into account fast and slow crops:

FAST CROPS	
Cutting lettuces	*4–5 weeks*
Radishes	*5 weeks*
Turnips (small)	*8 weeks*
Heading lettuces	*8 weeks*
Bunching carrots	*10 weeks*
Early peas	*10 weeks*
Kohlrabi	*10 weeks*
Courgettes	*10–12 weeks*
Early potatoes	*10–12 weeks*
French beans	*10–12 weeks*
Beetroot	*12 weeks*
Calabrese	*12 weeks*
Runner beans	*12 weeks*

SLOW CROPS	
Broad beans	*20 weeks*
Cauliflowers	*20 weeks*
Maincrop potatoes	*22 weeks*
Onions	*24 weeks*
Celery	*28 weeks*
Kale	*28 weeks*
Leeks	*28 weeks*
Brussels sprouts	*30 weeks*
Spring cabbage	*32 weeks*
Sprouting broccoli	*40 weeks*

YIELD CHART

Vegetable	Plant spacing in 1.2x2.4m (4x8ft) bed		Maximum number of plants	Average yield per 1.2x2.4m (4x8ft) bed	
	cm	in		kg	lb
Amaranth	15	6	133	9	4.5
Asparagus	60	24	8	8	4
Artichoke (globe)	45	18	14	7	3.5
Artichoke (Jerusalem)	37.5	15	18	35	17.5
Beans (runner)	15	6	133	22	11
Beans (broad)	15	6	133	9	4.5
Beans (round)	15	6	133	35	17.5
Beets (cylindrical)	20	8	75	50	25
Bok choi (pak choi)	20	8	75	30	15
Broccoli	30	12	33	16	8
Brussels sprouts	37.5	15	18	10	5
Bunching onions	20	8	75	15	7.5
Cabbage (round)	37.5	15	18	25	12.5
Cardoons	75	30	5	10	5
Carrots	10	4	300	35	17.5
Cauliflower	37	15	18	20	10
Celeriac	25	10	48	16	8

Vegetable	Plant spacing in 1.2x2.4m (4x8ft) bed		Maximum number of plants	Average yield per 1.2x2.4m (4x8ft) bed	
	cm	in		kg	lb
Celtuce	25	10	48	25	12.5
Chicory	10	4	75	15	7.5
Chinese broccoli	25	10	48	16	8
(gai lohn)	22.5	9	59	15	7.5
Collards	25	10	48	45	22.5
Corn salad	10	4	300	9	4.5
Corn (sweet)	30	12	33	11	5.5
Corn (dried)	37.5	15	18	6	3
Courgettes	60	24	8	35	17.5
Cucumber	37.5	15	18	30	15
(Daikon) radish	20	8	75	50	25
Dandelion greens	22.5	9	59	15	7.5
Eggplant	20	8	75	15	7.5
Endive	25	10	48	15	7.5
Florence fennel	25	10	48	16	8
Garlic	30	12	33	8	4
Good King Henry	37.5	15	18	8	4

NOTE: There are many variables that will affect plant yield, including weather, soil quality, insect damage, and variety growth. The average yields included in this chart are conservative ballpark figures for an intensive growing area with good soil quality. The weight listed represents only the edible part(s) of the plant.

YIELD CHART continued

Vegetable	Plant spacing in 1.2×2.4m (4×8ft) bed		Maximum number of plants	Average yield per 1.2×2.4m (4×8ft) bed	
	cm	in		kg	lb
Hamburg parsley	30	12	133	12	6
Horseradish	37.5	15	18	9	4.5
Kale	37.5	15	18	18	9
Kohlrabi	20	8	75	15	7.5
Leeks	15	6	133	60	30
Lettuce	20	8	75	18	9
Melons	45	18	14	12	6
Mizuna	15	6	133	15	7.5
Mustard greens	25	10	48	35	17.5
Spinach New Zealand	30	12	33	22	11
Okra	37.5	15	18	8	4
Onions	15	6	133	30	15
Parsnips	15	6	133	50	25
Peas (bush shell)	15	6	133	10	5
Peas (bush snap)	15	6	133	15	7.5
Peppers (sweet)	37.5	15	18	14	7
Peppers (hot)	37.5	15	18	4	2
Potatoes	30	12	33	19	9.5

Vegetable	Plant spacing in 1.2×2.4m (4×8ft) bed		Maximum number of plants	Average yield per 1.2×2.4m (4×8ft) bed	
	cm	in		kg	lb
Pumpkins	75	30	5	25	12.5
Purslane	15	6	133	6	3
Radicchio	20	8	75	12	6
Radish (round)	7.5	3	533	18	9
Salsify	20	8	75	37	18.5
Scallions	10	4	300	32	16
Scorzonera	30	12	33	15	7.5
Sea kale	40	18	14	8	4
Shallots	20	8	75	22	11
Spinach	15	6	133	14	7
Summer squash	60	24	8	40	20
Sunflower	45	18	14	12	6
Sweet potatoes	37.5	15	18	45	22.5
Swiss chard	22.5	9	59	25	12.5
Tomatoes	37.5	15	18	42	21
Turnips	22.5	9	59	22	11
Winter squash	60	24	8	18	9

VEGETABLE PLANNING CHART

The bar chart provides a visual guide to the time of sowing, transplanting, planting, growing, harvesting and storing vegetables, both protected and unprotected. It lists the vegetables in their plant families, which should greatly assist in deciding on the appropriate ground preparation, feeding, protection, and so on. This chart is available as a large format poster at www.ecodesignscape.co.uk

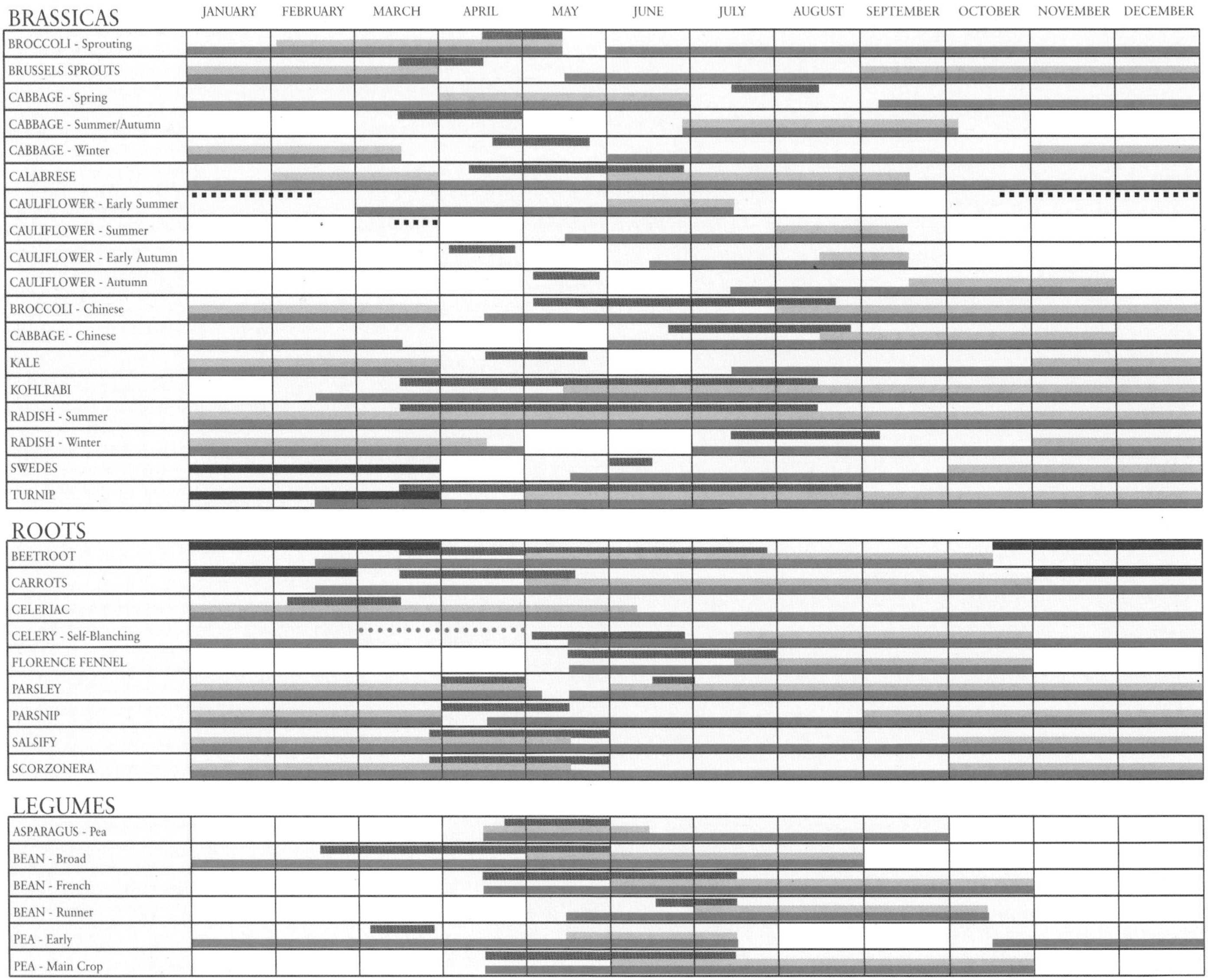

BRASSICAS	JANUARY	FEBRUARY	MARCH	APRIL	MAY	JUNE	JULY	AUGUST	SEPTEMBER	OCTOBER	NOVEMBER	DECEMBER
BROCCOLI - Sprouting												
BRUSSELS SPROUTS												
CABBAGE - Spring												
CABBAGE - Summer/Autumn												
CABBAGE - Winter												
CALABRESE												
CAULIFLOWER - Early Summer												
CAULIFLOWER - Summer												
CAULIFLOWER - Early Autumn												
CAULIFLOWER - Autumn												
BROCCOLI - Chinese												
CABBAGE - Chinese												
KALE												
KOHLRABI												
RADISH - Summer												
RADISH - Winter												
SWEDES												
TURNIP												

ROOTS	JANUARY	FEBRUARY	MARCH	APRIL	MAY	JUNE	JULY	AUGUST	SEPTEMBER	OCTOBER	NOVEMBER	DECEMBER
BEETROOT												
CARROTS												
CELERIAC												
CELERY - Self-Blanching												
FLORENCE FENNEL												
PARSLEY												
PARSNIP												
SALSIFY												
SCORZONERA												

LEGUMES	JANUARY	FEBRUARY	MARCH	APRIL	MAY	JUNE	JULY	AUGUST	SEPTEMBER	OCTOBER	NOVEMBER	DECEMBER
ASPARAGUS - Pea												
BEAN - Broad												
BEAN - French												
BEAN - Runner												
PEA - Early												
PEA - Main Crop												

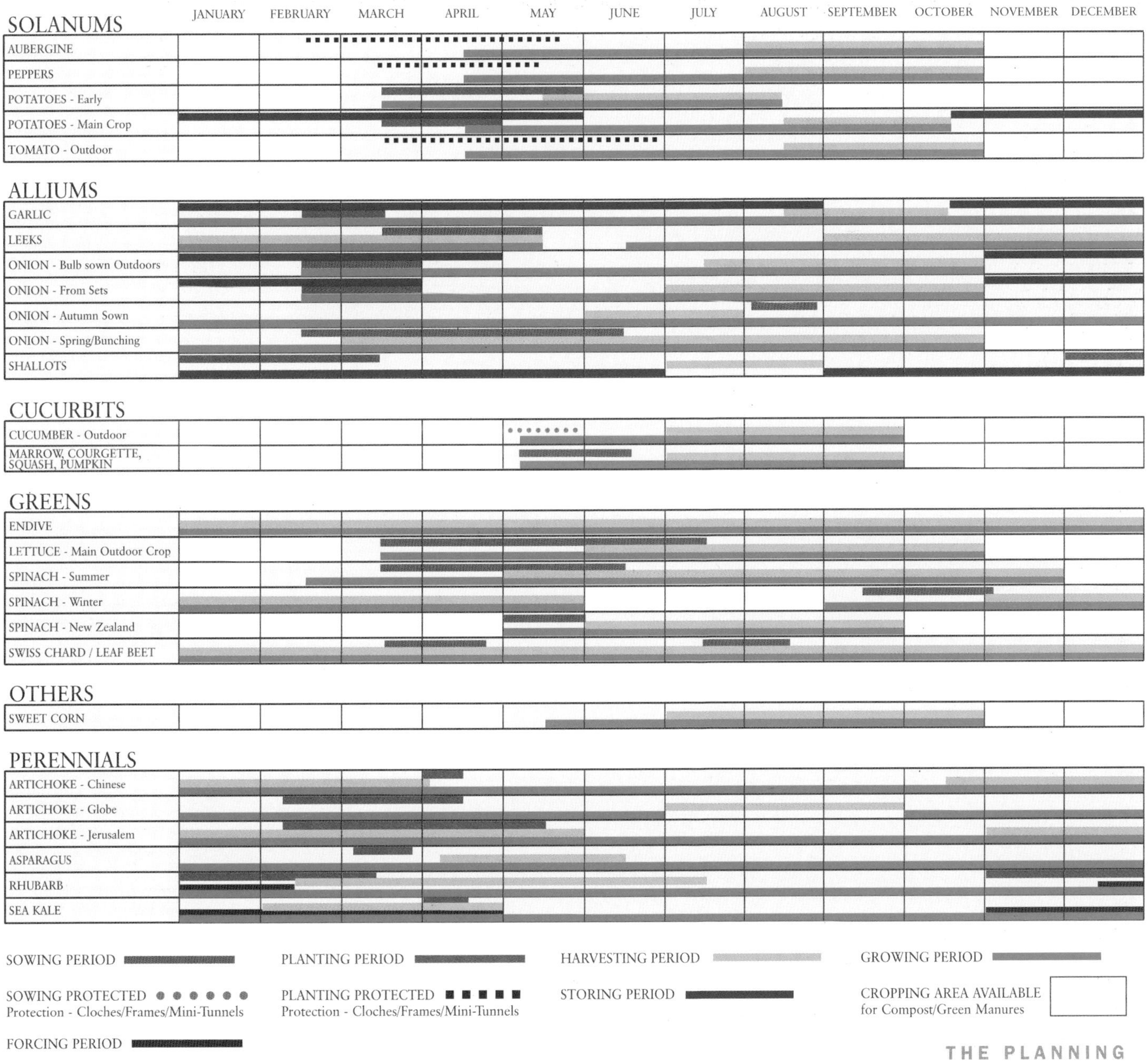

SOLANUMS	JANUARY	FEBRUARY	MARCH	APRIL	MAY	JUNE	JULY	AUGUST	SEPTEMBER	OCTOBER	NOVEMBER	DECEMBER
AUBERGINE												
PEPPERS												
POTATOES - Early												
POTATOES - Main Crop												
TOMATO - Outdoor												

ALLIUMS	JANUARY	FEBRUARY	MARCH	APRIL	MAY	JUNE	JULY	AUGUST	SEPTEMBER	OCTOBER	NOVEMBER	DECEMBER
GARLIC												
LEEKS												
ONION - Bulb sown Outdoors												
ONION - From Sets												
ONION - Autumn Sown												
ONION - Spring/Bunching												
SHALLOTS												

CUCURBITS	JANUARY	FEBRUARY	MARCH	APRIL	MAY	JUNE	JULY	AUGUST	SEPTEMBER	OCTOBER	NOVEMBER	DECEMBER
CUCUMBER - Outdoor												
MARROW, COURGETTE, SQUASH, PUMPKIN												

GREENS	JANUARY	FEBRUARY	MARCH	APRIL	MAY	JUNE	JULY	AUGUST	SEPTEMBER	OCTOBER	NOVEMBER	DECEMBER
ENDIVE												
LETTUCE - Main Outdoor Crop												
SPINACH - Summer												
SPINACH - Winter												
SPINACH - New Zealand												
SWISS CHARD / LEAF BEET												

OTHERS	JANUARY	FEBRUARY	MARCH	APRIL	MAY	JUNE	JULY	AUGUST	SEPTEMBER	OCTOBER	NOVEMBER	DECEMBER
SWEET CORN												

PERENNIALS	JANUARY	FEBRUARY	MARCH	APRIL	MAY	JUNE	JULY	AUGUST	SEPTEMBER	OCTOBER	NOVEMBER	DECEMBER
ARTICHOKE - Chinese												
ARTICHOKE - Globe												
ARTICHOKE - Jerusalem												
ASPARAGUS												
RHUBARB												
SEA KALE												

SOWING PERIOD

PLANTING PERIOD

HARVESTING PERIOD

GROWING PERIOD

SOWING PROTECTED
Protection - Cloches/Frames/Mini-Tunnels

PLANTING PROTECTED
Protection - Cloches/Frames/Mini-Tunnels

STORING PERIOD

CROPPING AREA AVAILABLE
for Compost/Green Manures

FORCING PERIOD

Monthly Harvest

	JAN	FEB	MAR	APR	MAY	JUN	JLY	AUG	SEP	OCT	NOV	DEC
Artichoke Jerusalem	■	■	■	■								■
Asparagus					■	■						
Beans, Broad						■	■	■				
Beans, French (bush)							■	■	■	■		
Beans, Runner								■	■	■		
Beetroot	■	■	■	■	■	■	■	■	■	■	■	■
Beetroot, leaves	■	■										
Broccoli, early & late sprouting	■	■	■	■	■							
Brussels sprouts	■	■	■									■
Cabbage, summer						■						
Cabbage	■	■	■	■	■		■	■	■	■	■	■
Carrots, early						■	■	■				
Carrots, maincrop	■	■	■	■	■			■	■	■		■
Cauliflower							■	■	■	■	■	
Celeriac	■	■	■									■
Celery	■			■			■	■		■	■	■
Celery, self-blanching											■	
Courgette								■	■	■		
Cucumber, outdoors								■	■			
Kale	■	■	■	■	■	■	■	■	■	■	■	■
Kohlrabi							■	■	■	■	■	
Lamb's Lettuce	■	■	■			■	■	■	■	■	■	■
Leeks	■	■	■	■	■				■	■	■	■
Lettuce	■	■	■	■	■	■	■	■	■	■		■

	JAN	FEB	MAR	APR	MAY	JUN	JLY	AUG	SEP	OCT	NOV	DEC
Marrows								F	F	F		
Onions, spring				F	F	F	F	F	F			
Onions	S	S	S	S	S	F	F	F	F	F	F	S
Parsley, Hamburg	F	F	F									F
Parsnips	F	F									F	F
Peas	S	S	S	S	S	F	F	F	F	F	S	S
Potatoes, early						F	F	F				
Potatoes, maincrop	S	S	S	S	S					F	F	S
Pumpkin	S	S							F	F	S	S
Radish, Chinese	F	F	F	F							F	F
Radishes					F	F	F	F	F	F	F	
Rhubarb			F	F	F	F						
Salsify	F	F	F							F	F	F
Salsify leaves				F								
Scorzonera	F	F	F							F	F	F
Spinach, summer					F	F	F	F	F	F	F	
Spinach, winter		F	F	F								F
Spinach, New Zealand							F	F	F	F	F	
Swedes	S	S	S									S
Sweetcorn	S	S	S	S	S	S		F	F	F	S	S
Tomatoes, outdoors								F	F	F	F	
Turnips	S	S	S									S

KEY: F = Fresh Crop; S = Stored (or frozen) Crop

CROP ROTATION

Crop rotation is a concept to be adapted to each individual garden. What is grown in a garden will, in the first place, be decided by the likes and dislikes of the gardener within the limits imposed by space and weather.

The smaller the garden the more impractical it becomes to follow a rotation plan rigidly, but the basic aims remain – to satisfy the manurial needs of each vegetable and to help it to resist pests and diseases.

The vegetables should be grown together in their respective plant families and in the crop rotation system. Continually growing any crops on the same piece of land will result in pests and diseases, soil sickness and poor yields.

Rotating the plant groupings, such as brassicas, legumes, roots, etc, will prevent the build-up of pests and diseases into damaging numbers and stop them from becoming established.

When related to the nutritional programme rotation is a means of maintaining soil fertility.

Leguminous crops, such as peas and most beans, add nitrogen to the soil; in traditional practice, legumes are followed by nitrogen-hungry brassicas. Alternatively one crop may exhaust the soil of certain nutrients it requires, but changing the crop will allow the soil reserves to be replenished.

Rotation can also be useful in weed control. Potatoes, for example, are a good crop for 'cleaning' the ground, partly because their dense foliage prevents weed germination, partly because earthing up in itself destroys weeds and exposes weed seed to birds. This makes them a useful crop to precede onions and carrots, which are difficult to grow in weedy ground.

Plant roots occupy different levels of the soil. Alternating deep- and shallow-rooting vegetables has a positive effect on soil structure.

The rotational plan can be on a three- or four-year basis. There is normally one plot in the garden that does not rotate, since certain plants, such as rhubarb, globe artichokes, asparagus, and so on, need a permanent position.

If many potatoes are grown, the vegetable garden can be divided into four, one part being given over entirely to potatoes. The vegetable cycle would then spread over four years instead of three, the peas and beans following the potatoes.

The general practice is to lime one-third of the garden where brassicas are growing because they seem to be more prone to club root, their most destructive disease, if the soil is short of lime.

Root vegetables often grow mis-shapen if they are given manure, so the ground they occupy in the rotation receives only a general fertilizer, there being adequate lime left from the previous brassica crop. Potatoes grown alongside the roots can be manured, but they must not have lime, because it may encourage scab.

Crops which follow other crops are usually called succession crops. Some are in fact quick-maturing catch crops which will be harvested before winter begins. Others, for example cabbages, will stay in the ground over the winter. Succession crops are not to be confused with successional sowings – sowings of the same vegetables at intervals in order to avoid a glut.

Cultivar Selection

Some vegetables, such as cabbage, carrot, cauliflower, leeks, lettuce, onions and peas, have a range of cultivars for different seasons; some can even be available to harvest all year round. Cultivars described as 'quick' or 'early' are especially useful at both the beginning and the end of the growing season, as they produce a crop more quickly than main crops. Others have been bred to tolerate cold conditions in winter.

Successional sowing

Successional sowing is another way of spreading the harvest, particularly suitable for fast-manuring crops. This means that small amounts of the same crop are sown at intervals of two to three weeks.

Green manures and Rotations

If copious quantities of farmyard manures are not available then using green manures in the rotation is a major bonus. Green manures add large quantities of organic matter to the soil, cover the soil, which helps to preserve structure, prevent erosion and keep down weeds, and hold nutrients in it over the winter. Some also fix nitrogen or access minerals and trace elements deep in the soil with their extensive root systems.

When growing green manures in the vegetable rotation, bear in mind that some of them are in the same plant families as vegetable crops. For example, fodder radish and mustards are members of the Brassica family, so should be included with the brassicas in the rotation. Field beans should only be grown in the legume part of the rotation.

Some green manures, such as alfalfa, need a whole growing year to be effective. Alfalfa is very deep rooting, bringing up nutrients to the surface, but the roots take a year to fully develop. It is only possible to fit alfalfa into a rotation if there is a bed free for the whole year.

Planning a Rotation

Plan the rotation according to the crops to be grown.

- Make a list of the vegetables to grow over a whole season and in roughly what quantities.
- Group vegetables together according to the botanical family.
- Vegetable families: Keep crops in the same family together (potatoes and tomatoes – both Solanaceae), moving them from plot to plot each year.
- Draw a plan of the growing area. Divide it into equal-sized sections according to how many years the rotation is to last. Fast-maturing crops can be fitted into gaps.
- Consider the 'Hungry Gap' period between late winter and early spring. Ensure space for sowing/planting in mid-late summer.

CROP ROTATIONS

Three-year Rotation Plan

A three-year rotational plan, the one most commonly used, allows each plot of plants with similar demands to change every year. This enables the plants to benefit from the previous crop and helps to keep pest and disease populations under control. A fourth plot P is for plants that do not like to be moved.

YEAR ONE

1	2	3
Asparagus pea Broad bean Celery Dwarf bean, Leek Lettuce, Onion Pea, Runner bean Squash Sweetcorn Tomato	Brussels sprouts Cabbage Calabrese Kale Kohlrabi Sprouting broccoli Swede Turnip	Beet Carrot Parsnip Salsify Scorzonera Potato

P: Asparagus, Globe artichoke, Jerusalem artichoke
Perennial herbs, Rhubarb, Seakale

YEAR TWO

2	3	1
Brussels sprouts Cabbage Calabrese Kale Kohlrabi Sprouting broccoli Swede Turnip	Beet Carrot Parsnip Salsify Scorzonera Potato	Asparagus pea Broad bean Celery Dwarf bean, Leek Lettuce, Onion Pea, Runner bean Squash Sweetcorn Tomato

P: Asparagus, Globe artichoke, Jerusalem artichoke
Perennial herbs, Rhubarb, Seakale

YEAR THREE

3	1	2
Beet Carrot Parsnip Salsify Scorzonera Potato	Asparagus pea Broad bean Celery Dwarf bean, Leek Lettuce, Onion Pea, Runner bean Squash Sweetcorn Tomato	Brussels sprouts Cabbage Calabrese Kale Kohlrabi Sprouting broccoli Swede Turnip

P: Asparagus, Globe artichoke, Jerusalem artichoke
Perennial herbs, Rhubarb, Seakale

Where space is limited, a three-year rotational plan allows each plot of plants with similar demands to change every year.

This enables the plant to benefit from the previous crop and helps to keep pest and disease populations under control.

A fourth plot is for plants that are considered permanent P

Four-year Rotation Plan

Divide the vegetables into the five groups (plots 1–5) shown in the table. Draw a plan to indicate which group of crops goes where, using a different colour for each group. (Remember, Plot 5 P is for the permanent crops.) Next year, move the crops in the next plot.

YEAR ONE

1	2	3	4
Broad bean Dwarf bean Pea Runner bean Squash Sweetcorn Tomato	Brussels sprouts Cabbage Calabrese Kohlrabi Sprouting broccoli Swede Turnip	Celery Garlic, Leek Lettuce Onion Shallot Squash Sweetcorn Tomato	Beet Carrot Parsnip Salsify Scorzonera Potato

P: Asparagus, Globe artichoke, Jerusalem artichoke
Perennial herbs, Rhubarb, Seakale

YEAR TWO

4	1	2	3
Beet Carrot Parsnip Salsify Scorzonera Potato	Broad bean Dwarf bean Pea Runner bean Squash Sweetcorn Tomato	Brussels sprouts Cabbage Calabrese Kohlrabi Sprouting broccoli Swede Turnip	Celery Garlic, Leek Lettuce Onion Shallot Squash Sweetcorn Tomato

P: Asparagus, Globe artichoke, Jerusalem artichoke
Perennial herbs, Rhubarb, Seakale

YEAR THREE

3	4	1	2
Celery Garlic, Leek Lettuce Onion Shallot Squash Sweetcorn Tomato	Beet Carrot Parsnip Salsify Scorzonera Potato	Broad bean Dwarf bean Pea Runner bean Squash Sweetcorn Tomato	Brussels sprouts Cabbage Calabrese Kohlrabi Sprouting broccoli Swede Turnip

P: Asparagus, Globe artichoke, Jerusalem artichoke
Perennial herbs, Rhubarb, Seakale

YEAR FOUR

2	3	4	1
Brussels sprouts Cabbage Calabrese Kohlrabi Sprouting broccoli Swede Turnip	Celery Garlic, Leek Lettuce Onion Shallot Squash Sweetcorn Tomato	Beet Carrot Parsnip Salsify Scorzonera Potato	Broad bean Dwarf bean Pea Runner bean Squash Sweetcorn Tomato

P: Asparagus, Globe artichoke, Jerusalem artichoke
Perennial herbs, Rhubarb, Seakale

Mini-rotation System

The cost in time and effort of growing vegetables can be high so it is essential to follow any ideas which can significantly increase the return. Using the bed system will greatly assist you in your efforts.

However, it does not always respond as well to the traditional crop rotation of dividing the area into three or four equal parts. By selecting which vegetables to grow and eliminating those that take up too much room, or demand too high a price in time and effort, it is possible to produce crops that will meet a much more convenient period of rotation for the gardener.

Bill Messer has produced a five-year plan as shown in the diagram below.

He abandoned the brassicas and then selected the most convenient period of rotation to cater for his crop selection. His layout consists of five beds measuring 1.2 × 9m (4 × 30ft), separated by paths 46cm (18in) wide.

Each bed goes through a five-year cycle but a year behind the one next to it, so that in any one year the range of crops produced is the same, but on different beds. Full details can be obtained from his article in *The Gardener*, August 1991.

Plot 1	Plot 2	Plot 3	Plot 4	Plot 5
Peas	Cabbages	Bulb onions	Potatoes	Rhubarb
Broad beans (fava) beans	Brussels sprouts Calabrese (Italian sprouting broccoli)	Spring onions (scallions)	Parsnips Beetroot (beets)	Asparagus Perennial herbs
French (green) beans Runner beans	Broccoli Kale	Leeks Garlic Sweetcorn (corn)	Beetroot (beets) Salsify Scorzonera	Globe artichokes Jerusalem artichokes
	Radishes Swedes (rutabagas or	Garlic Marrows (zucchini)	Celery Celeriac Tomatoes	Sea kale
	yellow turnips) Turnips	squashes and pumpkins		
	Kohlrabi	Lettuce		

WWII Cropping Plan

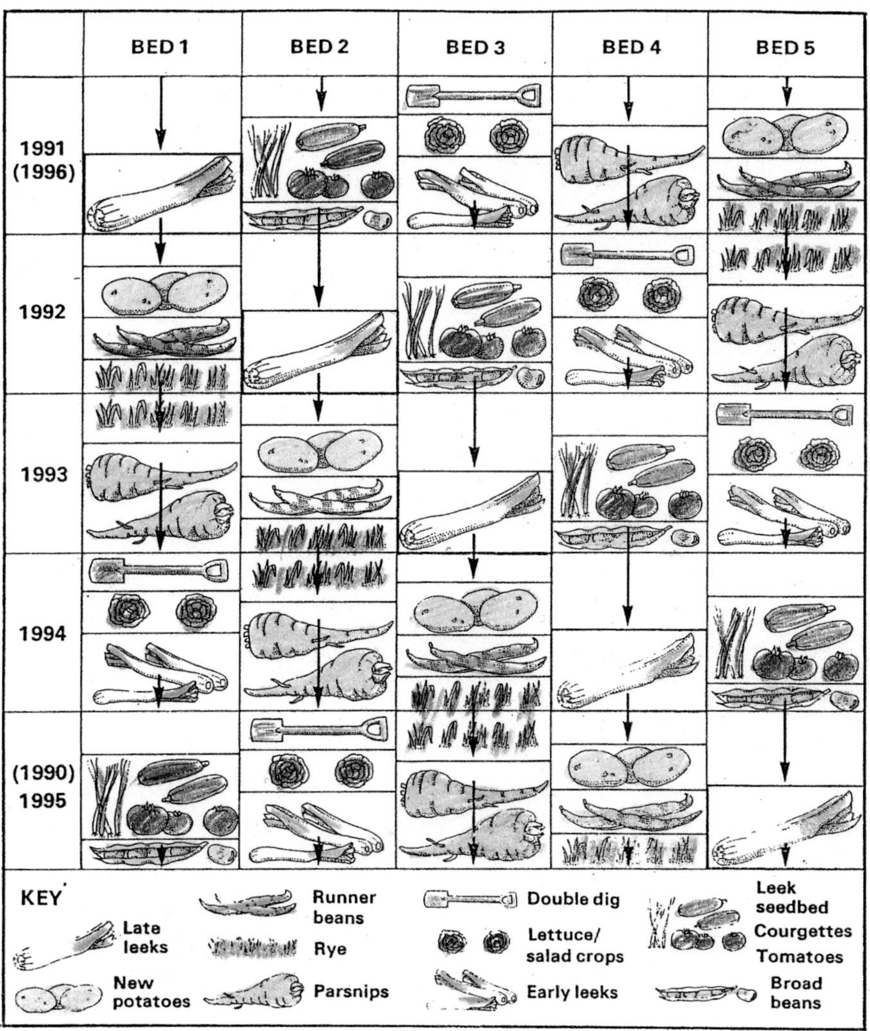

Acknowledgement: *The Gardener*

Monthly Greenhouse

Many vegetables can be raised in the greenhouse, pricked out into seed trays and hardened off before being planted in the vegetable plot. Seed packets provide valuable information on sowing times for individual varieties.

CROP	FEBRUARY	MARCH	APRIL	MAY
TOMATO Good Varieties Alicante Moneymaker Ailsa Craig Eurocross BB	If plants are to be grown in the greenhouse border, apply a light dressing of well-rotted manure or compost now and dig it in. A good dusting of general fertilizer is also beneficial.	Sow seeds in the middle of the month in pots or boxes of seed compost. Germinate in a temperature of 18°C (64°F) and prick out individually into 8cm (3in) pots when large enough to handle.	Keep the plants well supplied with water and remove any sideshoots as they form. Keep the greenhouse temperature between 13° and 16°C (55° and 60°F).	Early in the month plant either in the greenhouse border or in growing bags or large pots of John Innes No 3. Alternatively use ring culture method. Stake plants at the outset and space 45cm (18in) apart.
CUCUMBER Good Varieties Butcher's disease-resisting Improved Telegraph Fernspot Ferndan	Rig up training wires against the glazing bars where the cucumbers are to be positioned. They should run horizontally at 23cm (9in) spacings.	Cucumbers grown in soil borders in the greenhouse are best placed on a mound of manure topped with John Innes No 3. Make these mounds now, 30cm (1ft) high and 45cm (18in) wide.	Sow seeds, two to an 8cm (3in) peat pot of seed compost any time this month in a temperature of 18°C (65°F). Remove the weakest seedling after germination. Water the young plants generously. Do not allow to dry out. Temperature 16°C (60°F).	Plant out, making sure that peat pots are moist, either on mounds in large pots of John Innes No 3, or in growing bags. Tie the young plants in to the wire supports. Spray daily with tepid water.
SWEET PEPPER Good Varieties New Ace Early Prolific Worldbeater Canape	Sow seeds in pots or boxes of seed compost and germinate in a temperature of 16-18°C (60-65°F). Prick out individually into 8cm (3in) pots when large enough to handle, maintaining a temperature of 16° (65°F).	Sow seeds in pots or boxes of seed compost and germinate in a temperature of 16°C (60°F). Prick out individually into 8cm (3in) pots when large enough to handle.	Pot on into 15 or 20cm (6 or 8in) pots of John Innes No 3 or a soiless equivalent and keep the greenhouse at a temperature of between 16°and 18° (60°F and 65°F).	Stake the plants with small canes as they develop, and pinch out the growing tips when the plants are about 13cm (5in) high.
AUBERGINE Good Varieties Moneymaker Long Purple Black Prince Claresse		Water carefully and keep the plants warm.	Pot on into 13cm (5in) pots of John Innes No 2.	Pinch out the growing points when the plants are about 13cm (5in) high.
MELON Good Varieties Sweetheart Dutch Net Emerald Gem Charantais			Sow seeds in pairs in 8cm (3in) peat pots of seed compost and germinate in a temperature of 18°C (65°F). Remove weakest seedling after germination and maintain temperature at 16°C (60°F).	Plant the young melons either in growing bags or on mounds of John Innes No 3 on staging or borders. Equip each plant with a cane to take its growth up to the training wire.

JUNE	JULY	AUGUST	SEPTEMBER	OCTOBER
Water carefully. Remove sideshoots continually and tie in the stem as it grows. Feed plants as soon as first flowers open. Assist fruit setting by spraying with tepid water.	Keep an eye open for greenfly and whitefly and spray if troublesome. Continue feeding at weekly intervals. Harvest fruits regularly as soon as ripe.	Stop the plants when 5 or 6 trusses of fruit have been formed. Keep removing sideshoots. Check for pests and disease and combat when necessary. Carry on feeding.	Stop feeding and allow the plants a little less water to hasten fruit ripening.	Pick any fruits which are not ripe and store them indoors. Dig the plants up and consign them to the compost heap.
To prevent fruits from tasting bitter, remove all male flowers (those with very short stalks) before they open. All-female varieties will not carry any. Tie in shoots to wires. Stop sideshoots after two leaves have formed. Feed weekly.	First fruits can be picked this month as soon as ripe. Shade the house with blinds or whitewash. Top-dress plants when roots appear above compost.	Whitefly is a problem on cucumbers. Spray to control it as soon as it is seen. The same applies to red spider mite, though a moist atmosphere can keep this pest at bay.	Harvest the last fruits this month and clear out the plants and their compost.	
Spray the flowers with tepid water as they open so that the fruit is set. Feed every week with liquid fertilizer.	Keep an eye open for greenfly and whitefly and spray if they become a problem.	Harvest the fruits when green and plump. If they are allowed to turn red they are still edible but the plant will start to slow down as its fruits are ripening.	Continue harvesting and feeding.	Remove any fruit still on the plant and use them if they are large enough. Discard the plants.
Pot on into their final pots, 20cm (8in) in diameter. Use John Innes No 3 or a soilless equivalent. Spray plants against red spider mite and whitefly if these are a problem.	Spray the flowers as they open with tepid water to encourage the fruit to set. Feed every two weeks with liquid fertilizer. Allow only 6 or 8 fruits per plant.	Harvest the fruits when large enough and while they are still shiny. If allowed to become dull they lose their flavour and are tough. Pinch out all sideshoots to keep the plant's shape.	Continue harvesting and feeding. Discard plants when all fruit has been picked.	
Tie in stems to wires. Pinch out sideshoots when 2 leaves have formed. Allow only 4 or 5 fruits per plant. Remove a male flower and use it to pollinate all 4 female flowers on same day. Spray foliage with tepid water daily.	Feed with liquid fertilizer every 10 days after fruits have set. Stop main stem when it reaches ridge of house. Top-dress mound when roots appear above compost.	As melons swell they become heavy, so support them in net bags hung from wires. When fruits start to smell ripe, cut down on watering to prevent them splitting. Pick when ready.	Continue harvesting. Discard plants and clear away mounds when all fruit has been gathered.	

Cloche

The few minutes spent working out a programme for your cloches will make sure that they are utilized to their full extent. The suggestions below will help to keep them occupied all year round. Like those in the frame programme, any crops which need covering at the same time, for example, French and runner beans, can be interchanged.

	Jan	Feb	Mar	Apr	May	June	Jul	Aug	Sep	Oct	Nov	Dec
1				Sweetcorn								
						Melons						
										Broad beans		
2	Radishes											
				French beans								
						Sweet peppers						
									Peas: Meteor			
	Peas: Meteor (cont)											
3		Turnips										
				Runner beans								
						Melons						
	Lettuce: Imperial Winter (cont)									Lettuce: Imperial Winter		
4		Strawberries										
						Sweet peppers						
									Radishes			
5	Peas: Feltham First											
				Tomatoes								
						Melons						
										Lettuce: Kwiek		

Frame

The suggestions given here will help you plan a year's cropping in your frame. Any crops which occupy the same months can be interchanged, for example, melons with cucumbers. Either devote your whole frame to one programme or divide it into sections using a different programme for each.

	Jan	Feb	Mar	Apr	May	June	Jul	Aug	Sep	Oct	Nov	Dec
1	Carrots											
					Melon							
										Lettuce: Kwiek		
2	Vegetables for outdoor planting											
			French beans									
	Endive (cont)							Endive				
3		Turnips intercropped with radishes										
	Lettuce: Kloek (cont)									Lettuce: Kloek		
4	Vegetables for outdoor planting											
				Marrow								
	Lettuce: May Queen (cont)									Lettuce: May Queen		
5		Beetroot										
	Endive (cont)							Endive				
6	Vegetables for outdoor planting											
				Cucumber								
										Lettuce: Kwiek		

4 THE GROUND

- Soils
- Nutrients
- Fertilizers
- Minerals
- Compost
- Manures

SOILS

A Living Entity

Soil is a complex and diverse ecosystem. As with all such systems, it is a synthesis of the living and non-living components – living organisms, decaying organic material gases, water and mineral fractions. It is sensitive to change and, although capable of sustaining some degree of alteration, extreme pressure may cause a considerable loss of biodiversity. A soil ecosystem is a complex web comprising both that which is seen and that which is invisible to the eye. All of the elements, whether small or large, living or non-living, are interdependent. The loss of one constituent part may bring about changes, and these may, in the most extreme scenarios, culminate in the loss of the whole ecosystem and all of the life forms that it formerly supported.

Despite its credentials as a rich and complex ecosystem, much of what is written about soil in gardening texts is aimed at showing the gardener how to preserve the ideal structure, modify textural qualities, balance nutrients and manage water availability for plant growth. In fact, it is essential to realize that the soil resource is a living resource. It is a fragile and incredibly complex ecosystem, which, although capable of sustaining great change through pressure of usage, must be preserved at all costs.

The importance of microbes

Microbes are the driving force of the world's ecosystems, which can be seen as the 'eye of the needle' through which all soil organic matter must pass. In essence, as things die, they are broken down steadily until they are food for the very smallest soil inhabitants. From this point on they commence a process of re-assembly until they become part of the larger animals and plants in the soil, eventually passing on to us in the form of harvested produce. These microbes are often overlooked – they are so small that they are invisible to the gardener. Additionally, more than 95% of microbes cannot be cultured in a laboratory, making them difficult to study. As a result, scientists have (as yet) only uncovered the 'tip of the iceberg', and many species remain undiscovered.

The zone of soil adjacent to plant roots is the most ecologically significant. In healthy soil, microbes benefit appropriate species and may even be involved in the formation of symbiotic associations. In any case, the greatest numbers of microbes are found on the root surface with the relative occurrence decreasing sharply over a few millimetres, showing that both plant and microbes construe a mutual benefit by association.

One thing that should always be clear is that the majority of soil or organisms (both micro and macroscopic) require oxygen in order to survive. This, along with the microbes' often intimate association with plant roots, usually means that both plant roots and their associated soil organisms are limited to a fairly narrow band of the soil. Plants rarely root very deeply. Most of their rooting activity is limited to a fairly narrow layer of soil at the surface, often within 50cm (19in) of that surface. The most important layer is commonly referred to as topsoil, and is often characterized by a darker colour and a character that is different from that of the parent material immediately below.

The make-up of this living topsoil layer, which is so different from the more inert layers underneath, often surprises gardeners who assume it to be simply a growing medium. Good topsoil will consist of the following:

Volume as a Constituent Part Percentage of Total Soil Mass

1%	microbes
5%	plant roots
20%	air
25%	water
10%	dead organic matter
39%	mineral material (sand, silt or clay)

What do micro-organisms do for plants?

The chief role that microscopic organisms play is in the control of nutrient flow to plants. This may be direct, as in the case of symbiotic relationships such as nitrogen fixation by bacteria in root nodules on peas or beans, or indirect, as in more general nutrient cycling. Many cycles, including the carbon, sulphur and nitrogen cycles, are dependent on microbes during one or more parts of the process.

Microbes also benefit soils indirectly by detoxifying pollutants from both man-made or natural sources and keeping a healthy balance to the soil chemistry. In an average $1cm^3$ of healthy topsoil there are 90 million or more micro-organisms. Without these, none of the larger plant and soil organisms (and, indeed, ourselves, since all of our food comes from soil) would be able to survive. Look after these microbes and you are looking after the root of life itself.

Soil and Fertility

Soil is the garden's main raw material. The character of a soil cannot be altered, but regular cultivation and applications of organic compost, fertilizer and minerals will build up the fertility and reduce its deficiencies. Getting to know the soil type is an essential first step towards successful organic gardening.

Soil is divided into three main layers:

TOPSOIL
SUBSOIL
BEDROCK

There are however other layers between the top- and subsoils, as seen in the diagram.

The typical soil profile consists of a dark A. horizon rich in organic matter and humus, a heavier B. layer rich in minerals and a C. or subsoil horizon consisting of very heavy, often rocky soil. A layer of bedrock usually lies beneath the C level.

Topsoil can be improved by applying organic material to the surface. Subsoil can also be improved by the opening up of its structure through the application of sharp sand and fine gravels, and so on.

Typical soil profile

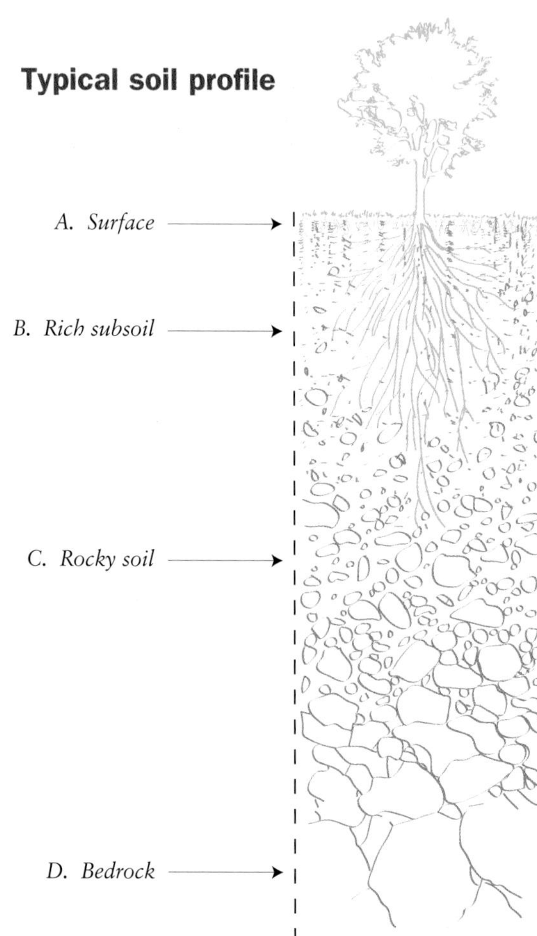

Soil check

SOIL TYPE	LOAM	CLAY	SAND	SILT	PEAT
STRUCTURE	Good – contains organic matter	Poor – requires soil particles to be opened	Very open	Good	Good
DRAINAGE	Good – retains moisture	Poor – add grit, sticky when wet	Quick – nutrients leach out easily	Fair	Fertile peat soils drain well. Others hold too much water.
TEMPERATURE	Warms up early Slow to freeze	Cold Quick to freeze Slow to warm	Suffers from drought Warms up early	Slow to warm Slow to freeze	Quick to warm
CULTIVATION	Do not work if wet.	Work soil only in dry weather.	Easy to work.	Work when soil is moist.	Any time
pH	Mainly neutral	Slightly acid	Often chalky and alkaline	Neutral to acid	Acid – sometimes very acid
ACTION	Maintain fertility by applying compost regularly.	Add bulky organic material/compost. Dig over and leave for frost action.	Requires copious amounts of organic matter. Keep soil covered at all times.	Needs compost on a regular basis.	Mix in bulky organic material.

Soil structure indicators

GOOD STRUCTURE	POOR STRUCTURE
Plant roots penetrate deeply	Plants are shallow rooting
Sweet, earthy smell	Unpleasant smell
Water does not sit long in the bottom of a hole after rain	Water sits in holes, or on the surface (below), or drains through immediately
Soil is relatively easy to dig	Soil is sticky, or in hard lumps, or very dry
No hard 'pan' – compacted layer – in the topsoil	Compacted layer in topsoil
Lots of worm channels	Few worms
Top layers are crumbly and friable when both wet and dry	Surface layer slumps when wet and dries out to a crust

Plants and Soil type

	PLANTS GROWING WELL	PLANTS NOT GROWING WELL
CHALK	Vegetables: peas, beans, brassica crops, chicory, many root crops if adequately watered in dry weather Fruit: all stone fruit, plums, gages, damsons, also peaches and nectarines if situation and climate are right	Vegetables: potatoes, swedes and other late-sown root crops, successional sowings generally if made in June or July Fruit: strawberries, raspberries, loganberries
CLAY	Vegetables: runner and broad beans, peas, the cabbage family, maincrop potatoes, short-rooted carrots and parsnips, globe beetroot, most summer salads not sown too early Fruit: apples, plums, maincrop strawberries, most soft fruit grown on bushes and canes	Vegetables: dwarf beans, long carrots, parsnips and beetroot, salads and vegetables sown in autumn and very early spring Fruit: dessert pears, peaches, nectarines, early strawberries
LOAM	All vegetables and fruits	Blueberries (peat)
SANDY	Vegetables: winter or early spring salad and vegetable crops, perpetual (winter) spinach, New Zealand (summer) spinach, long-rooted carrots, parsnips and beetroot Fruit: peaches, nectarines, figs, pears, bush and cane fruits if watered and mulched, early strawberries	Vegetables: summer lettuce, round-seeded spinach, summer cabbage, autumn cauliflowers, late crops of broad beans and peas Fruit: top fruits are often unhappy in dry summers, although small trees on dwarfing stocks are greatly helped by thorough watering and a thick peat mulch.

Acidity and Alkalinity

Soil Acidity

The majority of soils have a tendency to become acidic with time, except those derived from and overlying calcareous rock such as chalk. This is due to leaching – where rainfall exceeds evaporation. Water draining to groundwater naturally removes nutrients from the soil, including calcium, which is the main neutralizer of soil acidity. In time this can raise soil acidity levels considerably. In addition to leaching, rainwater naturally contains carbonic acid, sulphuric acid and nitric acid and within the soil itself, organic decomposition gives off organic acids (for example, acetic acid).

Despite this natural acidification effect, many soils remain alkaline and soils naturally range from highly alkaline to very acidic depending upon the local climate, their age, composition and parent materials. Most plants prefer or are tolerant of a specific pH range, although, generally speaking, good results may be obtained by maintaining soils at around pH 6.5-6.8.

The soil pH can actually affect the amount of nutrient that is available to the plant by affecting the balance of chemical reactions within the soil solution (soil water and dissolved chemicals). Where plants are grown in a soil that is not within their preferred pH range, a number of growth restrictions may occur, most of which are related to nutrient availability.

As soil pH lowers, for instance, nitrogen becomes limited – there is less nitrate available in the soil. Most nitrates are released from organic matter and, as the pH lowers, bacterial decomposition of organic matter decreases. Nitrogen requirements of plants at different pH levels vary as different plants exhibit varying tolerances/adaptations. Another major nutrient, phosphate, reacts with other chemicals within the soil and becomes unavailable outside the 6.5-7.5pH range. Some plants form relationships with soil-born fungi (*Mychorrhiza*), which release phosphates to plants in acid conditions.

Many trace elements are more soluble in acidic conditions, especially iron, aluminium and manganese and extreme acidity can lead to excessive quantities of trace elements and to the death of plants. Other trace elements, however, such as copper, boron and molybdenum, become less available at low soil pH, and deficiencies may occur. Molybdenum deficiency affects crops such as peas and beans. These will not grow well in acidic soils as the rhizobium bacteria that fix nitrogen in the root nodules do not work very well without molybdenum.

The acidity/alkalinity of a soil is measured on the pH scale (shown below), which very broadly indicates the amount of calcium in the soil.

pH Scale

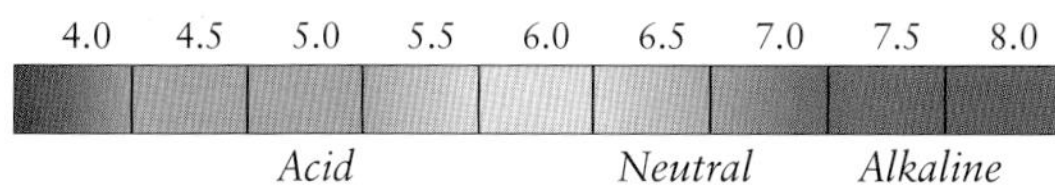

Changing the pH

More Alkaline:

Use ground limestone (calcium carbonate) or dolomite limestone (calcium magnesium carbonate).

Both are slow-acting and far better than slaked or hydrated lime, being less severe on the soil.

APPLICATION:

Apply in the autumn
Can take a full year to be fully effective
Rate depends on pH change required, generally 200g/sq m (7oz/sq yd) annually.

If magnesium levels are low, use dolomite limestone.

More Acidic:

Use composted pine needles or sulphur chips. Both slow-acting.

When to Apply Lime

Apply lime several weeks before sowing or planting. Ideally, dig manure into the soil in the autumn and lime in the spring. Never apply lime to soil that has just been manured because it will combine to form ammonia gas, which releases nitrogen into the air.

Do not lime an area where it is intended to grow tomatoes or potatoes the following season, as they are sensitive to excessive lime.

How much Lime

The amount of lime will depend to some degree on the soil type. Heavy clay soils need more than light sandy ones. As a rough guide, to increase the pH of a sandy soil by one unit, apply 1kg (2lb) lime every 100 sq m/yds. A sandy loam will need 2kg (4lb) for the same area, a medium loam about 3kg (6lb), and a heavy clay roughly 4kg (8lb). In practice, the pH level is not so critical that the plants are going to die if it is not exactly right. The pH levels recommended for specific plants in later chapters are intended as a guide only.

Types of Lime

Lime is available in several different forms. On the whole, the more expensive varieties, such as ground limestone or calcified seaweed, last longer in the soil.

Slaked lime (*Calcium oxide*)
Sometimes sold as 'garden lime', this is probably the most readily available. This is better than builder's lime (hydrated lime) because it lasts longer in the soil.*

Hydrated lime
Builder's lime, commonly sold for use with cement, is perfectly satisfactory for garden use but must be replaced at least annually.*

**Slaked and hydrated lime are NOT recommended for the organic gardener as they are soluble and quick-acting.*

Ground limestone

Often known as 'Dolomite lime', this is the best type to use. It is more expensive than hydrated or slaked lime but it will last in the soil for several years and it contains magnesium.

Calcified seaweed

This is in fact a type of coral. It is very useful because it contains magnesium and several other plant foods as well as lime. It lasts a long time in the soil – two to three years – but it is expensive. There is limited availability, as it is not a renewable resource.

Alkaline Soil

An alkaline soil can be brought closer to neutral by compost or manure on a regular basis. Compost has a buffering effect on the soil, correcting both acid and alkaline conditions.

Indicator Plants

Plants growing in a locality may provide the gardener with information about soil chemistry. Be aware that plants thriving in extreme soil types will also grow in more average soils so there should be a broad picture of both wild and cultivated areas.

- **Heavy clay/wet soil:** coltsfoot, horsetail (mare's tail)
- **Peaty/acidic soil:** corn spurrey, azaleas, rhododendrons, blueberry, corydalis, meconopsis. Blue hydrangeas retain their colour only on acid soils
- **Sandy, dry soil:** rock roses (Cistus)
- **Chalky soil:** ceanothus, hibiscus, rosemary, scabious, beech, clematis

Changing the pH

Quite acid pH 4.0 - 6.0	Slightly acid pH 6.0 - 7.01	Neutral to alkaline pH 7.0 - 7.5
VEGETABLES		
Chicory	Aubergine	Alfalfa
Dandelion	Beans	Asparagus
Endive	Buckwheat	Beet
Fennel	Mustard	Broccoli
Flax	Parsley	Brussels sprouts
Lupin	Parsnip	Cabbage
Marigold	Pea	Carrot
Potato	Pumpkin	Cauliflower
Radish	Soybean	Celery
Raspberry	Squash	Clover
Rhubarb	Tomato	Cucumber
Shallot	Turnip	Leeks
Sweet potato		Lettuce
Watermelon		Onion
		Silverbeet
		Spinach
		Swiss chard
		Zucchini/courgette
FRUIT		
Blackberry	Apple	
Blueberry	Apricot	
Watermelon	Cherry	
	Gooseberry	
	Grape	
	Peach	
	Pear	
	Strawberry	

NUTRIENTS

Nutrient Cycles

All the plant nutrients are in continuous circulation between plants, animals, the soil and the air. The processes contributing to the production of simple inorganic substances such as ammonia, nitrites, nitrates, sulphates and phosphates are sometimes referred to as **mineralization**. Mineralization yields chemicals that are readily taken up by plants from the soil solution. The formulation of humus, organic residues of a resistant nature, is known as **humification**. Both mineralization and humification are intimately tied up in the same decomposition process but the terms help identify the end product being studied. Likewise it is possible to follow the circulation of carbon in the carbon cycle, although these nutrient cycles, along with all the others, are interrelated.

Carbon cycle

Green plants obtain their carbon from the carbon dioxide in the atmosphere. During the process of photosynthesis, they are able to fix the carbon, converting it into sugar. Some carbon is returned to the atmosphere by the green plants themselves during respiration, but most is incorporated into plant tissue as carbohydrates, proteins, fats, and so on. The carbon incorporated into the plant structure is eventually released as carbon dioxide, (see the drawing).

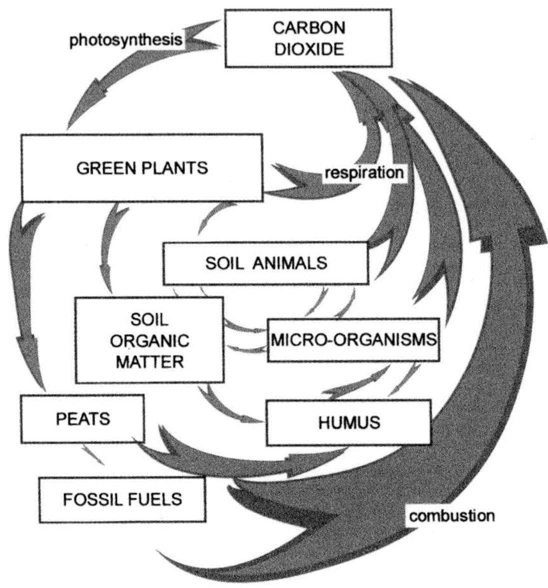

Carbon cycle: the recycling of the element carbon by organisms. Note how all the carbon in organic matter is eventually released as carbon dioxide by respiration or combustion. Green plants convert the carbon dioxide by photosynthesis into sugars which form the basis of all the organic substances required by plants, animals and micro-organisms.

Nitrogen cycle

Plants require nitrogen to form proteins. Although plants live in an atmosphere largely made up of nitrogen they cannot utilize gaseous nitrogen. Plants take up nitrogen in the form of nitrates and, to a lesser extent, as ammonia. Both are released from proteins by a chain of bacterial reactions as shown in the drawing.

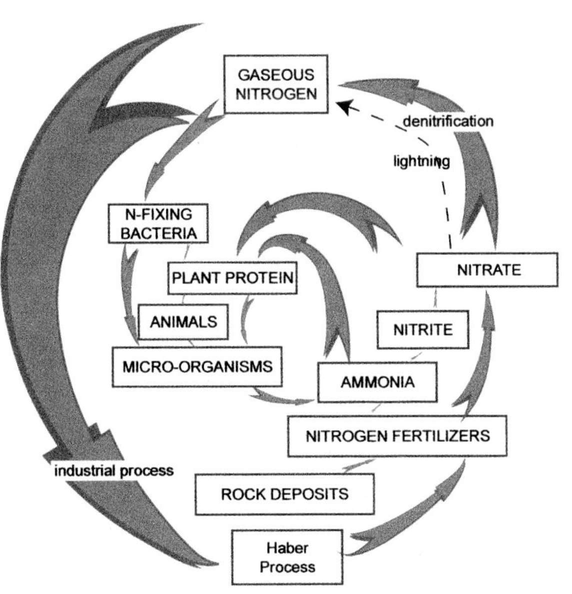

Nitrogen cycle: the recycling of the element nitrogen by organisms. Note the importance of nitrates that can be taken up and used by plants to manufacture protein. Micro-organisms also have this ability but animals require nitrogen supplies in protein form. Gaseous nitrogen only becomes available to organisms after being captured by nitrogen-fixing organisms or via nitrogen fertilizers manufactured by man. In aerobic soil conditions, bacteria convert ammonia to nitrates (nitrification), whereas in anaerobic conditions nitrates are reduced to nitrogen gases (denitrification).

Adapted from *Principles of Horticulture* by Adams & Early

Nutrient Cycles in a Typical Garden

Even small gardens contain nutrient cycles. Elements and nutrients are cycled repeatedly, both within the environment and as a result of the complex food chains and webs. This cycle of nature is essential in creating a balanced and healthy habitat.

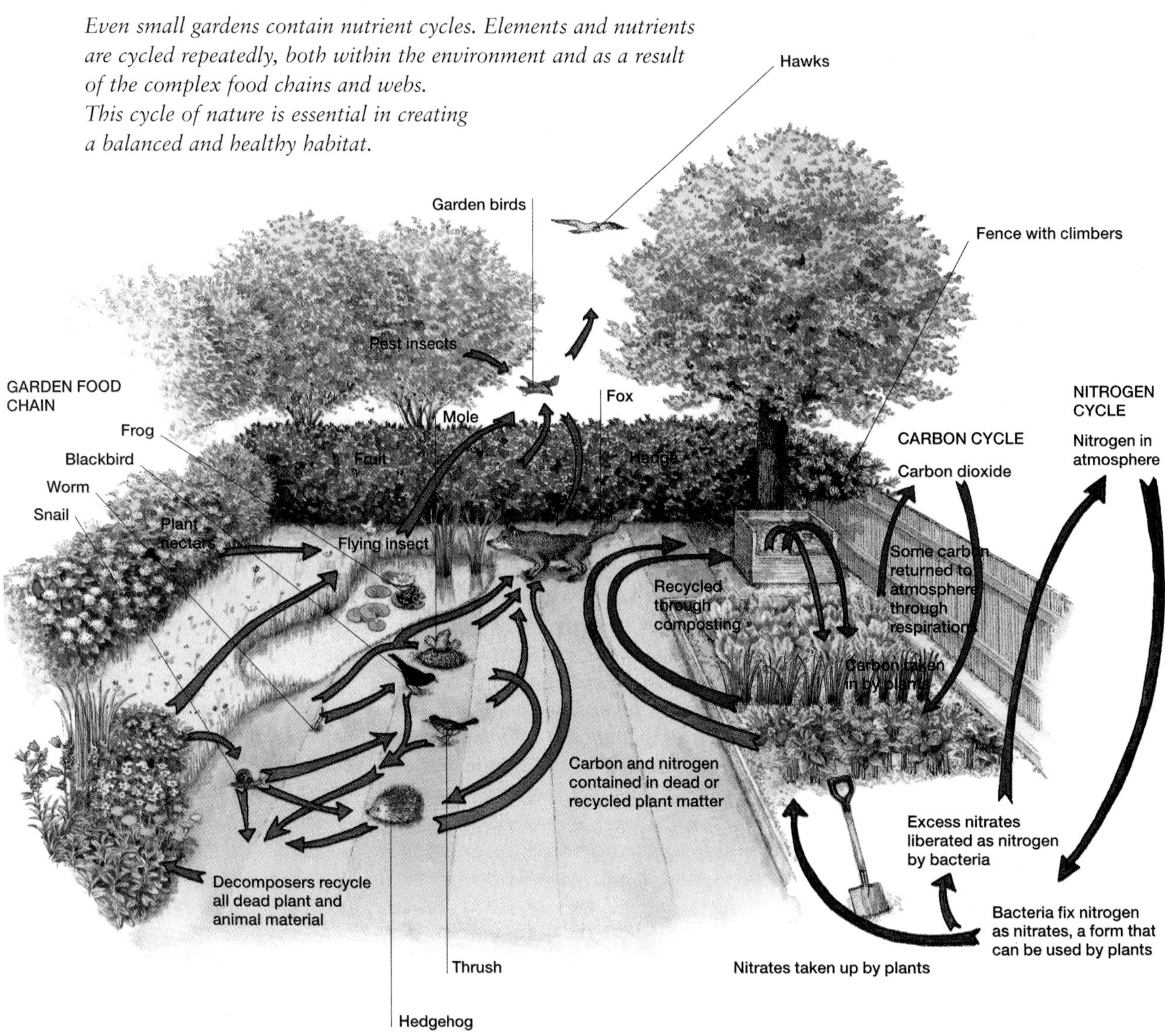

Plant Requirements

All plants require oxygen, carbon and hydrogen, which they obtain from the air, from sunlight and from water. They also need to obtain chemical elements found in the soil. These are divided into the major elements and trace elements. Oxygen, carbon and hydrogen are required in very large quantities whereas other nutrients are required in smaller amounts. However, it is essential to have specific proportions as too much of one can inactivate another; as an example, too much potassium can inactivate magnesium.

Proportions of elements required for healthy plant growth

Of the elements required for healthy plant growth, oxygen, carbon and hydrogen account for 96%–45% oxygen, 45% carbon, and 6% hydrogen. The nutrients described and some unspecified trace elements, make up the rest.

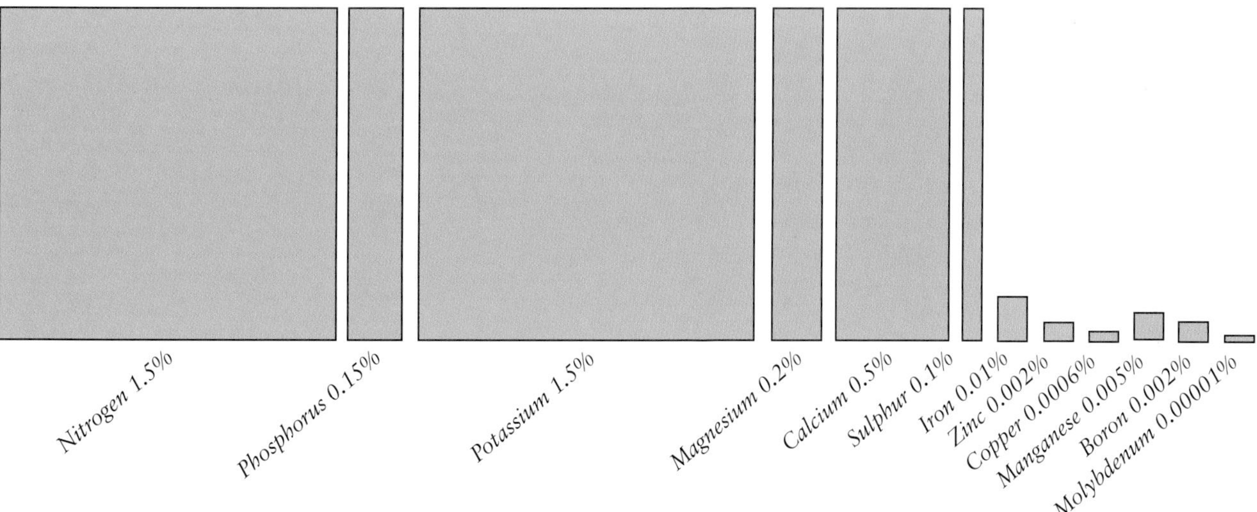

Major Elements

Nitrogen (N), phosphorus (P) and potassium (K) are the major elements needed in the largest quantities. They are present in all general fertilizers, some of which also contain magnesium (Mg). Most soils have adequate levels of calcium and sulphur, and these can be retained by regular additions of organic matter and by using good cultivation techniques.

Nitrogen (N)

One of the most important plant foods, nitrogen is a component of chlorophyll – the pigment that gives plants their green colour – and a vital part of the structure of plant protein. It is the element in the soil responsible for the vegetative growth of the shoots and leaves of a plant.

Deficiency is not unusual because nitrogen is easily lost by leaching in open soils and can be depleted by digging in unrotted material. If the soil contains insufficient nitrogen, plant leaves will become yellowed, particularly the older ones, and the plants will be stunted. Too much, on the other hand, will cause the plants to grow too quickly. There will be an abundance of 'soft' leaves and these may be a darker green than normal. The softer growth will be subject to attack by insects and by frost.

Nitrogen derives mainly from decaying organic matter, but also from the air via root nodules on legumes. It is the most likely of the main plant nutrients to become deficient, due to leaching. Plants respond most rapidly to applications of it, hence the widespread use of soluble nitrogen in conventional gardening. Excess can result in too much lush foliage development at the expense of flowering and fruit quality. It is also available in organic form, released by the action of soil bacteria, in well-rotted manures (rabbit, poultry, goat, horse, cow, in that order), compost, grass cuttings, which add humus content at the same time, as well as from legumes which make it available to other plants, green manures, and some of the organic fertilizers.

Phosphorus (phosphate P_2O_5)

The next most important element after nitrogen, phosphorus is needed in smaller quantities (only about one-tenth of the amount). Phosphorus, or phosphate, is mainly responsible for good root growth, so a deficiency causes slight stunting of the plant. It can be diagnosed by a distinct blue colour, affecting older leaves first. Sometimes the leaves darken and develop a blue/green tinge. In addition, the plant's root system is likely to be underdeveloped. It is available in soil organic matter, as well as in rock phosphate and phosphorus-rich organic fertilizers. Deficiency is more frequent in acid soils.

Potash (potassium, K_2O)

Potassium, required in the same quantities as nitrogen, affects the size and quality of flowers and fruit, and is essential for the synthesis of protein and carbohydrates. Potassium deficiency results in small, inferior flowers and fruit, and stunting of the plants themselves. It shows up, in older leaves particularly, as a yellowing around the edge of the leaves, followed by a brown scorching. Alternatively, the leaves may become bluish and eventually bronzed all over. An excess can result in plants not being able to take up magnesium and could cause an imbalance with other elements. Soil potash occurs almost entirely in mineral form, unavailable to plants. It is released by organic matter and is also available in very slow-acting rock potash and in the less delayed seaweed fertilizers and feeds. Deficiency is more frequent in sandy soils.

Minor Elements

Other plant foods (needed in small quantities)

Calcium

Required in relatively large amounts, calcium neutralizes certain acids formed in plants and helps in the manufacture of protein. Deficiency is rare in a well-managed organic garden, but plants sometimes develop an inability to distribute calcium through their system, although no one really knows why this occurs. The classic example is blossom-end rot in tomatoes, when the tip of the fruit blackens and rots. Lack of calcium also causes tip-burn on lettuce, black heart in celery and browning in the centre of Brussels sprouts. Deficiency will be most pronounced in young plant tissue.

Calcium is important for plant protein formation and cell structure. It is available in organic matter, ground limestone and dolomite, gypsum, mushroom compost, comfrey and some organic fertilizers.

Magnesium

Needed in much larger quantities than many gardeners realize, magnesium should be present in about the same quantities as phosphorus. It is also a constituent of chlorophyll so a deficiency causes yellowing, which starts between the veins of the leaves. The deficiency generally affects older leaves first.

A magnesium deficiency is sometimes caused by plants not being able to take up the magnesium in the soil, perhaps because there is too much potassium present. This can also happen if the soil structure is poor, with insufficient organic matter. Needed for plant uptake of other nutrients, it is available in organic matter and in seaweed. A deficiency can also be overcome with dolomite liming.

Sulphur

Sometimes classed as a trace element, sulphur is in fact needed in fairly large quantities. It forms part of many plant proteins and is involved in the formation of chlorophyll. Sulphur deficiency causes stunting and yellowing of the plant. However, the problem is rare since there is generally enough sulphur in organic soils because of the regular applications of compost and manure.

It is important to plant growth, particularly brassicas and legumes, and present in soils, as well as seaweed and gypsum.

Trace Elements

Although they are needed in very small quantities, these elements are none the less vital to plant growth. There are generally considered to be six of major importance: iron, zinc, copper, manganese, boron and molybdenum. Deficiencies are extremely rare because all the trace elements are present in manure, compost and the other bulky matter in the soil. However, problems can occur when the action of trace elements such as iron, manganese and boron is inhibited by alkaline, or limey, soil. This shows as a yellowing of rhododendron leaves and other acid-loving ornamental plants. Raspberries too are particularly susceptible to iron deficiencies, which show up as yellowing between the veins of the leaves.

Where deficiencies have occurred in the garden, the soil should be treated with seaweed meal fertilizer annually.

Iron

Small quantities of iron are required in the formation of chlorophyll. Symptoms of deficiency include yellowing between the veins of the leaves, especially the younger ones. It is more likely in alkaline soils and is sometimes confused with magnesium deficiency.

Zinc and copper

Both zinc and copper are enzyme activators, and a deficiency of either will lead to the same symptoms. Younger leaves in particular are mottled yellow, and citrus trees develop a condition known as 'little leaf', which is self-explanatory.

Manganese

This is necessary for the formation of chlorophyll and protein. Deficiencies are more likely to occur in alkaline soils, and will show up as a stunting of the younger leaves, and yellowing, especially between the veins.

Boron

This element is important to the growing tissue of all parts of the plant. Deficiencies are more likely to occur on alkaline soils and lead to a tissue breakdown. This causes internal 'corkiness', especially in apples and many root crops, and brown-heart in celery and brassicas such as cauliflower, broccoli and calabrese. (See Pests and diseases of vegetables.)

Molybdenum

A deficiency of this mineral, which is instrumental in the production of protein, will show up in deformed growth. It causes a condition called 'whiptail',which affects the cabbage (Brassica) family, and results in their leaves becoming thin and strap-like. Deficiency is generally due to acid soil conditions.

Chemical Symbols

Plant nutrients are commonly referred to by their chemical symbols – usually one or two letters – especially in the description of synthetic fertilizers, where the 'N:P:K' ratio is a prominent aspect of marketing.

Macronutrients

Nitrogen (N)
Phosphorus (P)
Potassium (K)
Magnesium (Mg)
Calcium (Ca)
Sulphur (S)

Micronutrients, or trace elements

Iron (Fe)
Manganese (Mn)
Copper (Cu)
Zinc (Zn)
Boron (B)
Molybdenum (Mb)

Symbols may also appear together to indicate chemical compounds – usually simply a common or more manageable form in which the nutrient can be applied. For example, rock phosphate may be written as P_2O_5, potash as K_2O and limestone, or calcium carbonate, as $CaCO_3$.

Treating Deficiencies

Treating an iron deficiency

Spray with liquid seaweed then apply a dressing of seaweed meal and/or manure.

Treating a zinc and copper deficiency

Apply a dressing seaweed meal, well-rotted manure or compost.

Treating a manganese deficiency

If rapid action is needed, spray with liquid seaweed then apply seaweed meal, manure or compost.

Treating a boron deficiency

Boron deficiencies must be prevented; once the symptoms of deficiency become apparent in a crop, it is too late to save it. Apply seaweed meal, manure or compost to ensure that the next crop will not suffer from the same problem.

Treating a molybdenum deficiency

Add lime to raise the pH of acid soil. Spray the plants with liquid seaweed fertilizer and apply seaweed meal and/or manure or compost to the soil.

Nutrient availability chart

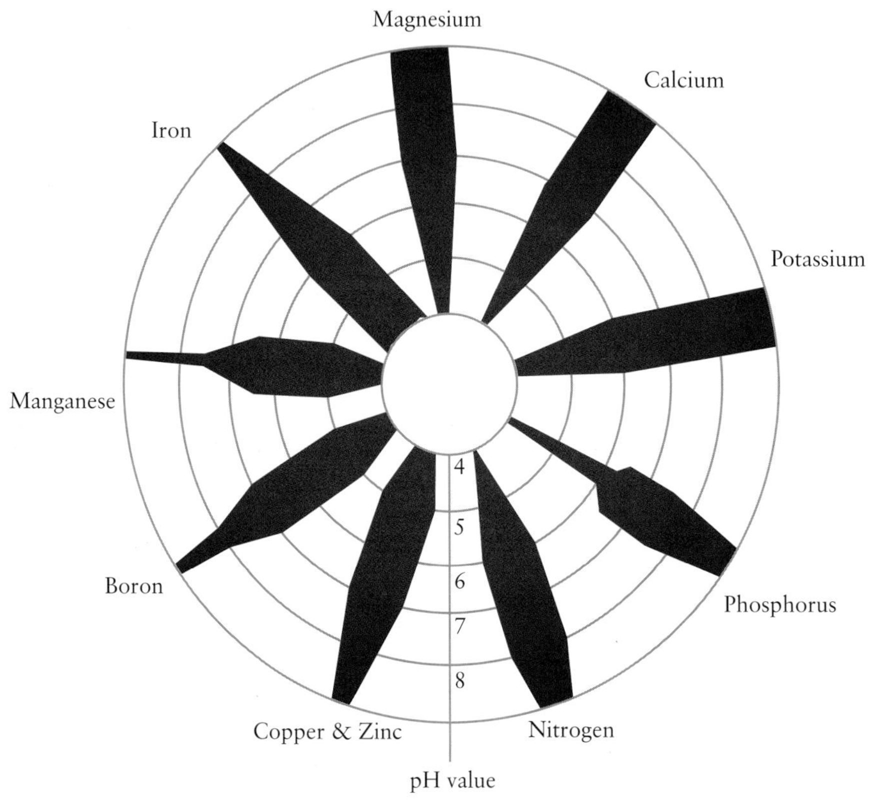

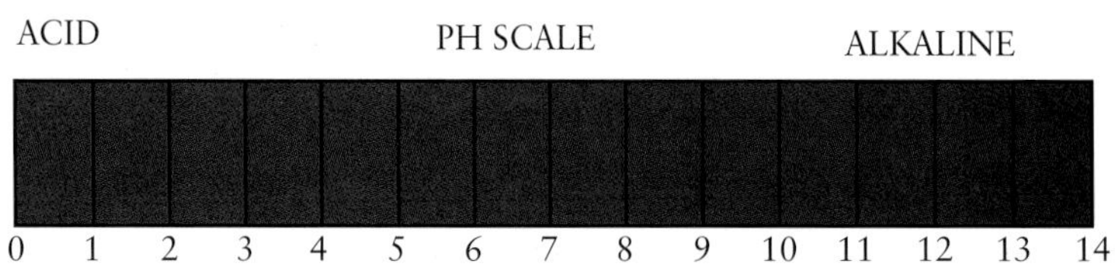

Plant Nutrient Guide

The following table highlights the characteristics of the soil nutrients. Symptoms of deficiency may be seen on different parts of the plant at different stages, although it may not always be immediately obvious that a plant is suffering from a nutrient deficiency. Some of the more important symptoms that can be identified on plants are listed below.

Major plant nutrients

PLANT NUTRIENT	NATURAL ORGANIC SOURCE	PLANTS MOST IN NEED	SOILS MOST IN NEED	SIGNS OF DEFICIENCY	HOW TO AVOID DEFICIENCY	TOXICITY CAUSE
Nitrogen (N) The 'leaf maker'	Dried blood, bird manure, blood and bone, grass clippings, legumes, stinging nettle, comfrey, tobacco stems and stalks, kelp, cattail reeds, coffee grounds	Grass, leaf vegetables grown for their leaves, and root-bound plants	Sandy soils in rainy areas	Stunted growth; small pale green leaves; weak stems, poor crop	Apply a base dressing before sowing or planting. Top-dress in spring and summer with organic matter. Use crop rotation to avoid depleting soil. Ensure adequate drainage to prevent soil becoming water-logged and sour.	Excessive use of nitrogen-rich fertilizer
Phosphates (P_2O_5) The 'root maker'	Comfrey, seagrass, bridal bower, marigold, chickweed, lemon balm, cottonseed meal, horse manure, fish, blood and bone, bonemeal	Young plants, root vegetables, and fruit and seed crops	Sandy soils	Stunted roots and stems; small leaves with a purplish tinge; low fruit yield, poor root development	Apply a base dressing of bonemeal or rock phosphate. Use fish, blood and bone when top-dressing and maintain an organically rich soil.	Excessive use of fertilizer
Potash (K_2O) The 'flower and fruit maker'	Comfrey, fennel, borage, stinging nettle, sow thistle, chamomile, yarrow, bark of all oaks, horse manure, seagrass, wood ash	Fruit, flowers and potatoes	Sandy soils	Leaf edges turning yellow, then brown; low fruit yield; fruit and flowers poorly coloured	Apply a compound organic fertilizer or wood ash as a base/top dressing or rock phosphate. Mulch plants with wilted comfrey or seaweed, or foliar feed with liquid comfrey or seaweed.	Excessive use of fertilizer; lack of magnesium

Minor plant nutrients

PLANT NUTRIENT	NATURAL ORGANIC SOURCE	PLANTS MOST IN NEED	SOILS MOST IN NEED	SIGNS OF DEFICIENCY	HOW TO AVOID DEFICIENCY	TOXICITY CAUSE
Boron (B)	Beetroot leaves, horse manure, compost, seagrass, untreated sawdust	Root vegetables, top fruit (apples, pears, and so on)	Sandy soils	Brown heart (roots); narrow leaves; corky patches on fruit	Top-dress with compost or apply borax in severe cases.	Irrigation water
Calcium (Ca)	Dandelion, lucerne hay, comfrey, horse manure, compost, blood and bone	Fruit, flowers, vegetables	Acid and potash-rich soils	Similar to nitrogen shortage: stunted growth and pale green leaves	Apply ground limestone or use gypsum or calcified seaweed.	High pH causes toxicity for some acid-loving plants
Copper (Cu)	Nettles, yarrow, horse manure, compost, blood and bone	Fruit, vegetables	Sandy soils	Dieback; brown spots on leaves	Top-dress with compost.	Copper-based fungicides
Iron (Fe)	Stinging nettle, compost, dandelion, horse manure, spinach and seaweed	Rhododendrons azaleas, camellias	Chalky, peaty, very light and acid soils.	Yellowing of younger leaves	Iron shortage in chalky soils is due to lock-up by calcium and difficult to avoid.	Rare
Magnesium (Mg)	Grass clippings, seagrass, mullein, sow thistle	Roses, tomatoes	Sandy, peaty and potash-rich soils	Yellow or brown patches between veins of older leaves	Apply dolomite limestone: maintain an organically rich soil. Apply compost mulch or Epsom salts if deficiency is severe.	None
Manganese (Mn)	Chickweed, compost, untreated sawdust	Rhododendrons, azaleas, camellias	Shortage in chalky soils is due to lock-up by calcium	Yellowing between the veins of older leaves	Acidification for some plants	None
Molybdenum (Mo)	Cornstalks, compost, grass clippings	Brassicas	Acid soils	Narrow leaves	Apply lime and top-dress with compost.	None
Sodium (Na)	Seaweed	Root vegetables, fruit	Sandy soils	Very rare except in a few seaside-loving plants	Not usually warranted.	Land reclaimed from sea
Sulphur (S)	Cabbage leaves, mustard, fennel, plantain	All plants	Soils in rural areas	Stunted growth and pale green leaves	A light dusting of flowers of sulphur during the year.	Industrial sites and acid rain
Zinc (Zn)	Horse manure, corn stalks, garden compost	Fruit, vegetables	Sandy soils	Dieback	Top-dress with compost.	Leaching from containers

Mineral Prospectors

Just as some plants can add nitrogen to the soil through root legumes, there are plants that can provide other elements by using them in building leaf and stem tissue. If they are allowed to grow in a particular spot, and then are pulled up, the minerals they have collected can be transferred from where they grew to where they are needed. These are two obvious advantages to be gained from using dynamic accumulators to extract excess minerals and to add extra minerals. In addition, some of these 'mineral prospectors' are able to 'fix' other raw elements to create mineral compounds for use by less talented plants.

Compost and Fertilizer Programme for Crop Rotation – Year One

PLOT ONE	PLOT TWO	PLOT THREE	PLOT FOUR
AUTUMN:	LATE AUTUMN/EARLY SPRING:	LATE WINTER:	LATE WINTER:
Add garden compost	Add manure, garden compost or mushroom compost	Add manure, mushroom compost or garden compost	Add manure or mushroom compost
SPRING:	SPRING:	SPRING:	SPRING:
Apply Seaweed meal, at 60 grms (2oz) per sq metre. Do not use lime or calcified seaweed. Feed plants with liquid seaweed (throughout season).	Apply lime or calcified seaweed 60 grms (2oz) per sq metre to ensure that the soil pHs levels 6.5-7.0. Cauliflowers may require additional feeding of liquid manure or seaweed during the growing season.	Apply seaweed meal if soil is not acid, at 60 grms (2oz) per q metre. Feed plants with liquid seaweed throughout the growing season.	Do not apply any calcified seaweed or lime. Add well rotted farmyard manure or mushroom compost when planting potatoes.
PLOT ONE BECOMES TWO THE FOLLOWING YEAR	PLOT TWO BECOMES PLOT THREE THE FOLLOWING YEAR	PLOT THREE BECOMES PLOT FOUR THE FOLLOWING YEAR	PLOT FOUR BECOMES PLOT ONE THE FOLLOWING YEAR
			This means autumn composting of plot one can be eliminated.

Organic Fertilizers

It should be stressed that organic fertilizers are 'slow release' and are not used for quick action. This is especially noticeable in spring, when nitrogen is required urgently by plants but the release of the nutrients cannot be achieved by micro-organisms until the soil has warmed up.

Organic fertilizers do supply nutrients over a longer period than artificial ones.

Organic fertilizers are less soluble than artificial fertilizers so less likely to be leached out of the soil. The rates of application are less critical, but they are relatively more expensive. They may supply minor elements, trace elements, and growth-promoting substances as well as major elements or nutrients, which is not the case with artificial fertilizers.

Organic Liquid Fertilizers

There are a number of approved organic products available only in liquid form. Some are seaweed extracts, others are made from cow slurry and farmyard manure. They are widely used to stimulate plant growth and supply some nutrients. Liquid feeds can also be made from comfrey (*Symphytum officinale*), which has a high potash content and is therefore a useful tomato fertilizer, stinging nettles and manure. In the main, these products are diluted and either watered on the ground or applied to plants as a **foliar feed**.

The advantage of liquid feeding is that, since plants can only take up nutrients in liquid form, the nutrients are available immediately; granular fertilizer has to be dissolved first. The disadvantage is that liquid fertilizer does not remain effective for as long as granular fertilizer and is leached into the subsoil fairly quickly. Liquid feeding is used to supply short-term nutrients to hungry plants and to correct deficiencies; it should not be considered as an alternative to solid feeding.

Foliar Feeding

This method involves spraying the leaves of the plant. It is faster acting but shorter lived than other methods so is really only of value for rapid remedial action when deficiencies are seen. Liquid seaweed sprayed on to leaves, for example, is something of a 'miracle cure' for trace element deficiencies. However, it should always be supplemented by feeding the soil with seaweed meal fertilizer as well.

Liquid Feeds or Fertilizers

- Feeds the plants directly.
- Provides plants with readily accessible nutrients.
- Boosts plant growth while the fertility of the soil is being improved.
- Acts as foliar feeds where plant roots are restricted.
- Can be made from animal manures, rock minerals and plants.
- May be made by the gardener or purchased ready made from specialist suppliers.
- Should only be used as a short-term solution.

Types

MANURES
Cow, sheep, poultry, fish

ROCK MINERALS
Rock phosphate is an example

PLANTS
Comfrey – high in potash
Nettle – low in phosphate, high in major elements, magnesium, sulphur and iron.

Note: both comfrey and nettle are slightly alkaline so not recommended for acid-loving plants. Horsetail is high in all soil nutrients and rich in silica.

Compost can also be used to make a liquid feed. Seaweed sustains chlorophyll levels, improves frost resistance and stimulates plants' immune system and resistance to pests and diseases.

Recipes for home-made Feeds

COMFREY
Soak 3kg of leaves in 45 litres of water. Cover with a lid. Use undiluted after four weeks.

NETTLE
Soak 1kg of leaves in 10 litres of water. Cover with a lid. Use after two weeks diluted one part to 10 parts of fresh water.

Application

LIQUID FEEDS (ratios, not absolute quantities or percentages)					
	N	P	K	Other	COMMENTS
Comfrey	2	3	5		*Foliar liquid feed, benefits soil structure, K especially good for fruiting crops*
Nettle	3	2	3	calcium, iron, silicon	
Seaweed	2-5	0.5	2.5	trace elements	*Foliar feed, useful to remedy trace element deficiencies; contains plant growth hormones assisting rooting and giving pest and disease resistance*
Manure	4	2	5		*Useful for fruit crops, tomatoes, potatoes*

Commonly used Fertilizers

NAME	FUNCTION	APPLICATION	NPK	COMMENTS
Bone meal	Good source of phosphorus.	100/135g/sq m 3-4oz/sq yd	6% N 15%P_2O_5	Mix into the soil. Lasts 6-12 months.
Dried blood	Quick acting source of nitrogen.	Liquid 50g in 1 litre.(2oz in 2pts)	12-14% N 2.5% P_2O_5 1%K_2O	Scatter around plants.
Fish, blood & bone meal	General fertilizer.	65-200g/sq m 2-6oz/sq yd	3.5% N 8% P_2O_5	Apply two weeks before sowing/planting or as top dressing during season.
Hoof & horn meal	Rich source of organic nitrogen.	135g/sq m 4oz/sq yd	14%N 2.5% P_2O_5	Slow release – not noticeable for first 4-6 weeks. Lasts up to 12 months. Use sparingly. Apply Spring and Summer.
Kelp meal & seaweed	Contains trace elements.	135/200g/sq m 4-6oz/sq yd	12% N 27%K_2O plus trace elements	Contains various compounds which encourages bacterial activity and plant growth. Hoe into soil during Autumn.
Fish meal	Good source of nitrogen and phosphorus.	135/200g/sq m 4-6oz/sq yd	3-3.5% N 20-30% P_2O_5	Lasts 6-8 months.
Wood ashes	Contains potassium, magnesium and calcium.	Apply thinly	0.1% N 0.1% P_2O_5 1% K_2O	Too much will make soil alkaline. Ideal for root crops. Deters slugs and root maggots. Lasts up to 6 months.
Compound		135-440g/sq m 4-12oz/sq yd		Various concentrated organic animal and vegetable waste products.

(All analyses are very approximate: N = Nitrogen, P_2O_5 = Phosphate, K_2O = Potash)

Vegetable requirements (Using fertilizer with 21% N content)

VERY LOW 12g/sq m (½ oz/sq yd)	LOW 23-35g/sq m (1-1¼ oz/sq yd)	MEDIUM 45-55g/sq m (1½ -2oz/sq yd)	HIGH 70-100g/sq m (2½ -3½oz/sq yd)	VERY HIGH 110g/sq m (4oz/sq yd)
Carrot	Artichoke	Artichoke (Jerusalem)	Beetroot	Cabbage (spring, summer, winter)
Garlic	Asparagus	Aubergine	Brussels sprouts	Broccoli (Chinese)
Radish	Beans (all)	Broccoli	Celery	Cabbage (Chinese)
	Celeriac	Broccoli (Sprouting)	Leek	Mizuna greens
	Chicory (all)	Cabbage	Potato (maincrop)	Pak choi
	Courgette	Calabrese	Spinach beet	Rhubarb (cutting years)
	Cucumber	Cauliflower	Swiss chard	
	Endive	Kales		
	Florence fennel	Lettuce		
	Kolhrabi	Potato (early)		
	Marrow	Pumpkin		
	Okra	Rhubarb (young)		
	Onions (all)	Spinach		
	Parsnip	Sweetcorn		
	Salsify	Sweet peppers		
	Scorzonera	Sweet potatoes		
	Spinach (New Zealand)			
	Swede			
	Tomato			
	Turnip			

Peas do not require any extra nitrogen.

MINERALS

Minerals can be supplied by plants, from substances found in the ground and even used sources. Plants are very good at accumulating large amounts of minerals and trace elements and can indicate the presence of a particular mineral. For example, nettles indicate a soil rich in phosphorus while clover grows well on soils that are deficient in nitrogen.

Substance	Function	Application	Comments
Basalt rock powder	High in phosphorus, potassium, calcium, magnesium and iron.	1–1.5kg (2–3lb) in a single application per 3sq m (30 sq ft)	Apply as result of soil test; lasts 4 years in soil after application.
Rock phosphate	Long-term source of phosphorus and some trace minerals.	1kg (2lb) in a single application per $3m^2$	Apply as result of soil test; lasts 3–5 years.
Colloidal phosphate	A soft, sedimentary material. An alternative to the harder rock phosphate. Has similar chemical properties.	1kg (2lb) in a single application per $3m^2$	Apply as result of soil test; lasts 2–3 years. Do not use with rock phosphate.
Granite dust	Long-term source of potassium. Released slowly.	Up to 750g (1.5lb)	Apply as result of soil test. Can also be used as a mulch. Lasts up to 10 years after application.
Greensand	Rich source of potassium and trace minerals.	Up to 750g (1.5lb) in a single application per $3m^2$ (30 sq ft)	Product should be greenish-blue. Do not mix with granite dust.
Chalk and shells	Long-term source of calcium, and some trace elements. Use as a liming agent to balance pH.	Sprinkle lightly on soil and work in well	Apply as result of soil test. Can also be used as a mulch.
Dolomite limestone	Contains both calcium and magnesium. Used to raise pH.	1–2.5kg (2–5lb) in a single application per $3m^2$ (30 sq ft)	Apply as result of soil test. Over-application can tie up nitrogen in soil. Do not add to compost.

Substance	Function	Application	Comments
Epsom salts	A soluble form of magnesium.	Weak solution	Apply where clear deficiency is indicated by yellowing between leaf veins.
Seaweed meal	Slow-acting long-term source of trace elements; helps to build up humus.	4–6oz/sq yd 120–180g/sq m	Apply on the surface and rake in up to 3 months before planting.
Gypsum	Rich source of calcium and sulphur. A soil amendment that is pH neutral.	Apply as result of soil test	Used to correct sodium levels. High pH soils may require calcium. Improves clay soils.
Rock potash	Released over one season.	4oz/sq yd 120g/sq m	Use to improve low fruit yield.
Soot	Fast acting.	4oz/sq yd 120g/sq m	Deters slugs, can scorch foliage and kill small plants.
Wood ash	Good source of potassium.	4oz/sq yd 120g/sq m	Can deter slugs.

Mineral Accumulators from plants

Mineral	Benefits	Source
Calcium	Promotes development of plant cell walls	Concentrated by buckwheat, *Matricaria recutita* (corn camomile), corn marigold, dandelion, fat hen, goose grass, melons, purslane and shepherd's purse.
Nitrogen	Promotes healthy foliage	Taken from the air (not the soil) and best accumulated with leguminous plants and by digging in any succulent seedlings in their first flushes of growth.
Phosphorus	Promotes healthy root development	Concentrated by fat hen, corn marigold, purslane, vetches and the weed *Datura stramonium* (thorn apple).
Potassium	Promotes healthy root development	Accumulated by several plants including chickweed, chicory, fat hen, goosegrass, plantain, purslane, thornapple, sweet tobacco and vetches.
Silica	Promotes disease resistance	Made active by plantains, couch grass, stinging nettles and horsetails (*Equisetum*).
Sulphur	Promotes disease resistance	Accumulates in *Allium* (onion family), brassicas, fat hen and purslane. Can deter slugs.

Feeding

If there is high soil fertility there should be no need to feed the soil with fertilizers and minerals, as long as a good quantity of well-made compost is applied on a regular basis. Fertilizer is a supplement, not a replacement for compost. However, there may be a need to add fertilizer to boost the major elements for plant growth – nitrogen, phosphorus and potassium (or NPK). Occasionally, trace elements or minerals may be lacking. Iron deficiency on very acid soils and phosphorus deficiency on very acid soils is not uncommon. If necessary, send off for a full soil analysis to pinpoint the problem.

Other reasons for fertilizing are when crops need a boost. The exact amount and which type of feed depends on the plants, and whether the aim is to improve the fruit and flower, or increase leaf growth, for example.

The standard practice, used until the soil is fully fertile, is to apply a top dressing of an all-round fertilizer such as blood, fish and bone or seaweed meal prior to planting. Liquid fertilizers are used to perk up plants in containers where nutrients may be running out, or for a quick boost for failing specimens.

COMPOST

A fertile and rich growing soil has to be the dream of every gardener and allotment holder, and there are many ways in which it can be achieved. Garden centres and nurseries have bags of organic matter piled high, all claiming to represent the secret to gardening success. Whilst many of these will be every bit as good as the packaging claims, they have all been produced elsewhere, packaged and transported – all of this uses energy such as fossil fuels. It may seem a small undertaking, but the more gardeners recycle and limit inputs from outside, the more sustainable their actions become. Gardeners have sometimes become too reliant on purchased items and it is often well within their own grasp to make a wonderful soil conditioner that will feed the army of microbes in the soil and ultimately form the basis of a self-sustaining soil fertility. Making compost is free and is also without cost for the wider environment.

Fertile soil is the most important element in growing healthy vegetables and fruit, and the way to achieve fertile soil is by incorporating large amounts of organic matter, via the compost system.

The combination of animal and plant wastes with dry matter such as straw and hay plus seaweed ensures that a compost of good quality is made. Everything should go through the composting system, just as nature intended it to.

There is a danger in applying manures directly on to edible plots due to the complexity of animal feeds – be they fresh or dry – unless they are from an approved organic farm.

Applying compost after it has been properly made will ensure that the worms have plenty of food. They will also assist in the creation of soil structure that retains moisture and is well drained. The microbiological activities below ground level are of the utmost importance.

Every organic gardener should ensure that the soil receives priority of care when ground becomes vacant and, if no compost is available, then green manures should be grown.

It is essential to keep the ground well covered or mulched at all times to protect the soil, which is a very important long-term investment.

For nutrient-rich compost materials, the following list may help in a general way. Remember, though, that a plant's needs cannot be served with one or two materials alone as nature loves a harmony of many parts. Make compost accordingly. Collect the materials when they are as fresh as possible. Avoid any that have been sprayed with poisons. Wash the salt off those that come from the sea or seashore. These precautions will ensure the continuing vitality of the compost heaps and the soil in the garden.

The use of ample organic manure is fundamental to the success of most vegetable gardens, and especially to those newly created on sandy or clay soils. Organic matter provides food for plants, especially nitrogen and phosphate. Sandy and light chalky soils are improved because the humus holds more water and clay soils are made more easily workable.

Compost Activators

To encourage the start of the composting process it is essential to use a material that encourages biological activity:

- Nettle (exclude roots)
- Urine
- Comfrey (exclude flowers)
- Manure
- Seaweed
- Horsetail (exclude roots)
- Fertilizer such as dried blood or bonemeal
- Seaweed (granules or powder).

Compost Materials

SUBSTANCE	FUNCTION	SOURCE	COMMENTS
Weeds	Provide raw green matter for good general fertility; high in nitrogen	From fields or gardens	Do not use weeds that have gone to seed or contain seeds; shred and chop weeds before use if possible.
Grass clippings	Provide raw green matter for good general fertility; high in nitrogen	Gardens (if not sprayed)	Spread fresh clippings thinly to avoid matting and unpleasant smell; best used for mulching after 1–2 days' drying time; use only clippings free from any chemicals.
Rotted hay (mulch hay)	Improves soil structure and general fertility	Farms	Difficult to work into the soil unless well rotted; compost over the winter to make mulch hay.
Brewery waste, spent hops	Good source of nitrogen	Breweries	Brewery waste breaks down quickly, spent hops more slowly; compost well before using, since fresh material may lower soil pH in beds.
Coffee waste, chaff, and grounds	Balanced source of mineral nutrients	Household waste, coffee-processing plants	Compost well before using, since an excess of grounds may make soil too acidic for some plants.
Peanut, buckwheat, or rice hulls	Improves soil structure and general fertility	Food-processing plants	High in potassium; also contains other plant nutrients.
Nut or cocoa shells	Used for soil building and maintenance; rich in mineral nutrients	Chocolate factories, nut-processing plants	Shells should be ground up and sprinkled on as other materials.
Shredded newspaper	Improves soil structure and adds carbon	Recycling centres	Do not use papers printed with coloured inks.
Sawdust	Improves soil structure and produces humus	Sawmills, timber yards	Must be well rotted when mixed into the soil, or it will tie up soil nutrients, making them unavailable to plants; compost before applying. Allow to rot in heap.

Compost Materials continued

SUBSTANCE	FUNCTION	SOURCE	COMMENTS
Wood shavings	Improves soil structure and produces humus	Sawmill, timber yards	Fresh shavings can tie up nutrients in the soil, so compost before applying. Shavings, especially from hardwood, can take more than 2 years to compost sufficiently. Allow to rot in heap.
Straw	Improves soil structure and produces humus	Available in bales at farms and farm-supply stores	Fairly coarse but decomposes rapidly; best used chopped, with other materials such as grass clippings.
Cornstalks	Improves soil structure and produces humus; stalks are good source of many nutrients	Cobs and stalks available from farms in autumn after field corn has been harvested or milled	Compost material over the winter before applying in the spring; if applied fresh, it can tie up nutrients in the soil. Use at base of compost heap. Best if chopped.
Vegetable wastes	Improves general fertility	Supermarkets and restaurants; kitchen and market gardens	Avoid adding any bones or grease along with vegetable wastes; process in a compost pile before using.
Fruit wastes	Improves general fertility	Fruit-processing plants, organic or home orchards, cider mills	Peels and skins are especially high in minerals; avoid chemically sprayed fruits; process in a compost pile before using.
Dry leaves	Improves soil structure; an excellent source of many mineral nutrients	Lawns, parks, landscape and public gardens	Cover leaves with soil or a tarpaulin to keep them from blowing away; oak leaves may be acidic unless composted; compost any leaves to make leaf mould, which may be added to garden at any time of year. Keep these separate from compost heaps in their own container made from wire netting to make leaf mould. This can then be mixed in with other compost materials or used as a mulch.

Carbon to nitrogen ratio

All nutrients play a part in all nutrient cycles simply because all organisms need the same range of nutrients to be active. Normally there are adequate quantities of nutrients, with the exception of carbon or nitrogen, which are needed in relatively large quantities. **A shortage of nitrogenous material would lead to a build-up in the nitrogen cycle, ie the decomposition of organic matter is slowed because the micro-organisms concerned suffer a shortage of one of their essential nutrients. A useful way of expressing the relative amounts of the two important plant foods is in the carbon to nitrogen (C:N) ratio.**

Nitrogen is released during decomposition if the organic material has a C:N ratio narrower than 30:1, such as young plant material, or with nitrogen-supplemented plant material such as FYM.

In general, fresh organic matter decomposes very rapidly, as long as conditions are right, but the older residues tend to decompose very slowly.

Carbon to Nitrogen (C:N) RATIOS

Apple pomace	21:1
Bonemeal	3·5:1
Bracken	48:1
Clover, flowering phase	23:1
Clover, vegetative phase	16:1
Compost, finished	16:1
Corn stover	60:1
Cottonseed meal	5:1
Fish scraps	4:1
Grain hulls and chaff	80:1
Grass clippings, dry	19:1
Grass clippings, fresh	15:1
Hay, legume/grass mix	25:1
Hay, mature alfalfa	25:1
Hay, young alfalfa	13:1
Leaves, dry	50:1
Leaves, fresh	30:1
Manure, chicken	7:1
Manure, cow	18:1
Manure, horse	25:1
Manure, human	8:1
Manure, rotted	20:1
Newspaper	800:1
Ryegrass, flowering phase	37:1
Ryegrass, vegetative phase	26:1
Sawdust, hardwood	400:1
Sawdust, rotted	200:1
Sawdust, softwood	600:1
Seaweed	19:1
Straw, oat	48:1
Straw, wheat	125:1
Urine, human	0·8:1
Vegetable wastes	12:1
Vetch, fresh hairy	11:1

Data from
Designing and Maintaining Your Edible Landscape – Naturally
by Robert Kourik

MANURES

Animal Manures

It is not possible to state the exact nutrients for each of the manures since they vary according to the animal's diet; whether the manure is mixed with straw, sawdust or other organic material, and if it has been kept under cover or exposed to the elements. All manures contain some N (Nitrogen), P (Phosphorus) and K (Potassium), plus other useful elements. The figures given (as percentages) are only rough guides as to their relative nutritional values.

For reasons of health it is better to obtain organic manures. If none are available, do check out the source none the less.

All manure should be aged in heaps before it is used near the roots of any plants.

MANURE	DESCRIPTION	NPK
PIG	Rich but not volatile, so may be applied in a fresher state, preferably in spring and early summer. Excellent for the onion family, but caution must be used these days as pig diets are high in copper and this can be present in the manure at toxic levels, or at least will lock up nutrients	N 0·5 P 0·2 K 0·7
POULTRY	Should be used with caution as it is especially high in nitrogen and phosphates; also a useful source of sulphur, magnesium and lime. The nitrogen is often volatile (making a smell of ammonia) and is best conserved by adding the manure to the compost heap or blending with other manures. When applied direct to the soil, use very sparingly, 1/2-1lb/sq yd (220-440g/sq m)	N 1·7 P 0·6 K 1·2
COW	Least rich in terms of NPK and usually not volatile. Best composted before application and most suitable for light soils whose water retention will be considerably increased	N 0·4 P 0·2 K 0·4
HORSE	The best all-rounder: activates compost heaps, makes hot-beds and lightens heavy soils. Always compost before spreading. Some gypsum mixed with the heap will help to lock in volatile ammonia and thus conserve the nitrogen	N 0·6 P 0·4 K 0·7

MANURE	DESCRIPTION
RABBIT	Very rich source of nitrogen; contains many other plant nutrients and trace minerals. Best used in compost pile or to make liquid manure tea; improves soil structure and general fertility; avoid using fresh, since it can burn plants
SHEEP AND GOAT	Good source of many nutrients and trace minerals. If mixed with bedding, can be difficult to work with until it has decomposed; compost before use
PROPRIETARY BRANDS	Made of composted animal manure, these can be used where the original manures are in short supply. They are concentrated and expensive, so use sparingly. Do not use them as potting composts as the levels of NPK can be too high and/or imbalanced for seedling plants

Other sources of Nitrogen

PRODUCT	DESCRIPTION
LEATHER DUST AND LEATHER SCRAP	Rich source of nitrogen. Use as a supplemental source of nitrogen in the first year garden or with heavy feeder crops like corn and cabbage
FEATHERS	Good source of nitrogen; not a good structure-building material. Shred and compost feathers before adding to beds
WOOL WASTE	Good source of nitrogen and other nutrients. Avoid using dyed or contaminated wool waste
HUMAN HAIR	Rich source of nitrogen; contains other nutrients and trace minerals. Excellent resource for urban gardeners; may discourage some animal pests such as rabbits and deer when spread thinly around plants in garden; compost before adding as a soil amendment

Green Manures/Cover Crops

Many plants (known as 'green manures' in the UK or 'cover crops' in the USA) greatly assist the organic gardener by providing a very economical means of improving soil fertility.

Benefits

- Improves soil structure
- Replaces soil nutrients
- Increases humus content
- Protects the soil surface
- Eliminates weeds from vacant land
- Many plants provide nitrogen
- Attracts beneficial insects
- Provides winter soil cover
- Can be sown spring to autumn
- Provide short- or long-term ground cover
- Certain species can be grown between or under rows of vegetables, such as sweetcorn
- Many plants are deep-rooting

Sowing

Choose a variety to suit conditions and requirements.

Seeds are sown in closely spaced rows or broadcast.

Clovers require a good level of calcium in the soil for optimum growth and very often they are sown with a nurse crop such as annual ryegrass.

Vetches (tares) can be sown with winter grazing rye.

Digging in

Plants can be dug in to the ground or the top vegetation can be cut and harvested for use in compost making.

With leguminous plants it is better to leave the roots in the ground to decay. Most plants should be used before flowering.

Incorporating the green manure into the soil must be done in the right way if the maximum benefit is to be obtained.

Do not let the crop become too woody before it is dug in or the rotting process will take nitrogen from the soil. If the crop is fairly large, cut it up finely before cultivating the soil. This can be done with a rotary mower or, with lower-growing crops such as mustard, even a cylinder mower.

Allow a period of wilting before digging the material under. Low-growing crops can simply be cut down with a spade and allowed to wilt for a few days, then dug in. Taller plants can be worked into the surface with a rotary cultivator and then, after a few days, rotavated more deeply.

Do not bury the material deeper than about 15cm (6in). If the crop has become hard and woody, it may be necessary to apply liquid fertilizer to assist rotting. Watering over with liquid seaweed or animal manure should suffice.

Problems

- Several green manures release compounds harmful to seed germination when they are turned in, so let them rot down before digging them into the soil
- Some green manures such as fodder and mustard are brassicas so should only be grown in that part of the rotation. Similarly, field beans belong to the bean family and rye grasses are in the same family as sweetcorn
- Never let a green manure flower unless it is required to attract pollinating insects, as nitrogen will be lost to the flower and resulting seed head. The exceptions are those plants, such as alfalfa, clover and trefoil, which are grown for more than one season
- There are some green manures that need a long season to be beneficial. Crops such as alfalfa could be difficult to incorporate in a rotation unless there is space available
- Beware of under-sowing green manures too early as they can outgrow vegetables

Mulching

- Green manures can be hoed, cut or mowed down and the foliage left on the surface as a mulch.

Green Manure Guide - Winter

These species can withstand moderate to hard frost for a long period and can be cut down in the spring, prior to cultivation. The shorter species can also be used as catch (cover) crops around winter vegetables or biennial crops for harvest in the early spring. This protects bare soil, prevents nutrient leaching and creates a more stable soil environment.

PLANT	SOWING TIME	SOWING RATE	NITROGEN FIXING?	TIME IN GROUND	HEIGHT	BULK QUALITY	DEEP-ROOTING?	DIGGING IN	SOILS	NOTES	TYPE
Alfalfa (Lucerne) *Medicago sativa*	Apr-Jun	3g ($^{1}/_{10}$ oz) per sq m (yd)	Yes – but poor	3–24 months	100–150cm (3–5ft)	Good	Yes	Any time. Medium effort if young, hard if left for more than one season	Will grow on most soils.	Very deep-rooting. Drought resistant. Extremely useful in the garden as long as there is space to let it occupy land for a whole season. Provides plenty of green matter.	HP
Alsike clover *Trifolium hybridum*	Apr-Aug	3g ($^{1}/_{10}$ oz) per sq m (yd)	Yes	3–24 months	30cm (12in)	Moderate	No	Any time. Medium effort	Dislikes acid or waterlogged soils	Prone to drought. Shallow-rooted. Good for nitrogen. A good clover for heavy or wet soils.	HA
Broad or fava bean *Vicia faba*	Mar-Apr Sep-Oct	150cm apart	Yes	Spring 2–3 months Winter 5–6 months	45cm (18in)	Moderate	No	As required	Will withstand wetter soils than other clovers	Excellent green-manure crop in every way. Will stand the winter almost everywhere. Produces plenty of organic matter, is a nitrogen fixer, and the beans can be harvested and eaten.	HA
Essex or red clover *Trifolium pratense*	Apr-Aug	3g ($^{1}/_{10}$ oz) per sq m (yd)	Yes	3–24 months	40cm (16in)	Moderate	No	Any time. Easy, little effort	Most soils Prefers good loamy soil	Can be mown or cut several times per season and used for compost. A low-growing nitrogen fixer with an extensive root system that will supply plenty of organic matter, red clover is best sown in spring or late summer.	HA

PLANT	SOWING TIME	SOWING RATE	NITROGEN FIXING?	TIME IN GROUND	HEIGHT	BULK QUALITY	DEEP-ROOTED?	DIGGING IN	SOILS	NOTES	TYPE
Grazing rye *Secale cereale*	Aug–Oct	15g (1/2oz) per sq m (yd)	No	6–8 months	30–60cm (12–24in)	Good	No	Before flowering. Hard work Pre-flowering.	Grows in most soils	A non-legume which has an extensive root system and produces a useful amount of green material to dig in and produces a good top growth. Keep watered during germination and sow thickly to smother weeds.	HA
Phacelia *Phacelia tanacetifolium*	Mar–Sept	3g (1/10 oz) per sq m (yd) or thinly in rows 20cm (8in) apart	No	2–6 months	60–90cm (12–36in)	Good	No	Hard work Any time.	Grows in most soils	Quick to grow in summer with good-quality top growth. If left, will produce mauve flowers that bees love.	HA
Trefoil *Medicago lupulina*	Mar–Apr	3g (1/10 oz) per sq m (yd).	Yes	3–12 months A/B	30–60cm (12–24in)	Moderate	No	Medium effort	Will grow in most soils but dislikes acid	Can be used for undersowing. Has dense foliage.	HB
Winter tares *Vicia villosa*	Mar–May July–Sep	200g/sq m 15g/m^2	Yes	Spring 2–3 months Autumn 5–6 months	50–75 cm	Good	No	Any time before flowering	Avoid acid and dry soils	A tall plant that is one of the most useful crops because it grows during winter when land is vacant. Sow in rows, as for lupins, during late summer and dig them in in early summer.	HA

TYPE HA = Hardy Annual HP = Hardy Perennial HB = Hardy Biennial HHA = Half-Hardy Annual

Green Manure Guide - Spring/Summer

Plants for use in the spring and summer have to be quick-growing in order to cover the ground and yield benefit within a short period of time. They are generally slightly tender, although lower-growing species can actually be used as a catch crop around other seasonal crops.

PLANT	SOWING TIME	SOWING RATE	NITROGEN FIXING?	TIME IN GROUND	HEIGHT	BULK QUALITY	DEEP-ROOT?	DIGGING IN	SOILS	NOTES	TYPE
Buckwheat *Fagopytum esculentum*	Apr–Aug	10g (2/5oz)/sq m (yd) or thinly in shallow rows 20cm (8in) apart	No	2–3 months	80cm (32in)	Good	Yes	Before or during flowering. Easy, little effort	Grows on poor soils	Useful only where space is available for the whole summer. Tall, with a very extensive root system. Makes copious organic matter but does not fix nitrogen. Also has the advantage that, if allowed to flower, it attracts hoverflies, which eat greenfly and aid pollination of crops.	HHA
Crimson clover *Trifolium incarnatum*	Apr–Aug	3g (1/10 oz)/sq m (yd)	Yes	2–5 months	30–60cm (12–24in)	Moderate	No	Before flowering. Medium effort	Prefers sandy loam soil but will tolerate heavy clay	Its large red flowers attract bees.	HA
Fenugreek *Trigonella foerumgraecum*	Apr–Aug	5g (1/5oz)/sqm(yd) or thinly in 15cm (6in) shallow rows	No	2–3 months	30–60cm (12–24in)	Good	No	Any time before flowering. Easy, little effort	Prefers good drainage tolerates heavy or light soil		HHA
Fodder radish	Aug–Sep	50g/m^2	No	10 months	30cm	Good	Yes	Spring	Well-drained	Has a deep tap root.	HB
Italian ryegrass *Lolium* species 'Westerwolds'	Mar–Apri	10g/m^2	No	Spring 3 months Autumn 6 months	30cm	Moderate	No	Before seed heads appear	Suitable for most soils	Fast-growing and bulky, a good crop for sowing early in the spring. Will germinate quickly, even in cold soils, and can be dug in even before the ground has warmed up sufficiently to plant out tender vegetables. It is essential to use the annual strain ('Westerwolds') rather than the perennial or biennial ryegrass, which will cause endless problems by re-growing, and that it is dug in before it produces seeds.	HA

PLANT	SOWING TIME	SOWING RATE	NITROGEN FIXING?	TIME IN GROUND	HEIGHT	BULK QUALITY	DEEP-ROOT?	DIGGING IN	SOILS	NOTES	TYPE
Lupin *Lupinus angustifolius*	Mar–Jun Mar–Sept	4cm (1½in) deep; 3cm (1¼in) apart; in rows	Yes	2–3 months	50cm (20in)		Yes	Pre-flowering. Easy, little effort	Prefers light, slightly acidic soil	Foliage not very dense. Deep-rooting plant that adds nitrogen and phosphates to the soil.	HHA
Mustard (white) *Sinapsis alba*		15cm (6in) apart 5g/m2	No	1–2 months	60–90cm (24–36in)	Good	No	Pre-flowering	Moisture-retentive fertile soil	A quick-growing, short and shallow-rooting crop that will make plenty of organic matter for digging in and act as a good weed suppressant. Used widely in gardens where land cannot be spared for long. It has a big disadvantage in that it is a member of the cabbage family, so it could harbour club-foot.	HHA

TYPE HA = Hardy Annual HP = Hardy Perennial HB = Hardy Biennial HHA = Half-Hardy Annual

5 THE PLANTING

- Sowing/Planting
- Cropping
- Plant Spacing
- Growing Media
- Vegetable Growing Guide
- Lunar Gardening
- Pollination
- Watering

SOWING/PLANTING

Direct Outdoors

Depending upon the location, the crop, the season and other circumstances, vegetable seeds can be sown directly in the ground where they will not be disturbed until they mature.

To achieve optimum results with a deep bed, it is essential that the soil is loose and dug deeply, so that the roots can penetrate to the required depth, and that it is enriched with plenty of organic matter. Treading on the bed once it has been dug will compact the soil. If it is too awkward to work across the access paths, use a wooden board to spread your weight evenly over as large an area as possible.

Outdoor Seedbed

Seeds can be sown in a specially prepared bed in relatively close rows from which young plants can be lifted and transplanted into their permanent positions.

Direct Under Cover

Seeds, such as quick-growing salad crops, can be sown direct in the ground that has been prepared with the appropriate growing media. They should then be protected, be it in a glasshouse, cold frame or cloche.

Successional Sowing

Successional sowing, as the name suggests, is the practice of sowing seeds of the same crop, several times over at regular intervals. There are several advantages to doing this. It is chiefly done to extend the cropping season for 'quick season' crops whose harvest season is relatively short once mature. Many summer salad crops come into this category; lettuces in particular are prone to 'bolting' (producing a flower stem) if they are not harvested promptly. Successional sowing may also be useful where crops are sown directly outdoors, early in the season where they may be prone to frost damage. Early crops can be sown under cover (for example, under a cloche) where they will begin to develop earlier

Crops suitable for successional sowing	
Beetroot	Spring to summer
Broccoli	Spring to summer
Cabbages	Spring to summer
Carrots	Spring to summer
Endives	Spring to summer
Kohlrabi	Winter to spring
Lettuce	Winter to spring
Parsnips	Winter to spring
Peas	All year round
Potatoes	Spring
Radishes	Winter to summer
Salad leaves	Spring to autumn
Salad rocket	Spring to autumn
Spinach	Spring to summer
Spring onions (scallions)	Spring to autumn
Swedes	Spring to summer
Swiss chard	Spring to summer
Turnips	Winter to spring

than would otherwise be possible. Subsequent sowings outdoors will mature later and the season is again effectively extended. Many vegetables can benefit from this treatment and it is especially useful in colder areas where later sowing cannot otherwise guarantee a full season of cropping.

Successional sowing can also be practised with crops that are sown indoors. Vegetables can be raised under glass earlier in the year, and the crops may be gradually moved outdoors later in the year.

Gardeners with small plots can practise successional sowing by only sowing a short length of drill at any one time. This process is then repeated a week or so later, with further sowings as often as you like. This is a good way of having fresh vegetables for several weeks and avoiding a sudden glut.

CROPPING

Intercropping

Intercropping is the cultivation of two or more crops simultaneously on the same bed, where one crop is much faster-growing than the other. For example, fast-growing crops such as carrots, radishes and lettuce may be planted among slower-maturing ones such as cabbages, peas and potatoes.

Intercropping has certain similarities with companion planting but it is not specifically done for this purpose. Intercropping involves harvesting the quicker-growing crop first, before the slower-growing one achieves total foliage cover of the soil or area in which the other crop is growing. A good example of this is the sowing of a crop of spring onions or lettuce between a row of tomatoes. Similarly, spinach or radishes can easily be planted out early between sweetcorn or, alternatively, radishes can be planted out between cabbages.

Intercropping at its simplest is a means of increasing productivity, by ensuring that no space is left unused and by making the maximum use of the available light, nutrient and moisture. It will also reduce the amount of weed growth, due to the shading effect on the soil.

Ensure rows are wider apart to allow for sufficient space, light and moisture for each crop to develop.

Allow room for cultivation and harvesting. Avoid intercropping with naturally sprawling vegetables such as potatoes, courgettes, and so on, as they will engulf smaller plants in the vicinity.

In a slight variation on the theme, a green manure can be combined with the crop. This can be useful in the case of winter crops because the green manure doubles up as a cover crop, protecting the soil from leaching and erosion and actually stabilizing the soil temperature. Leguminous green manures planted among leafy winter crops such as cabbage or Brussels sprouts can provide nitrogen benefits throughout the remaining growing season. When the plot is dug in the spring, it will also provide a nitrogen boost to the young plants. It is certainly a system that can boost the productivity of an area but one that requires careful planning.

Succession planting information for Fresh Harvest

Vegetable	No. of added succession plantings in 8-month period	Harvest period (in weeks)	Plants per person for each planting
Amaranth	6	3	10
Asparagus	1	8	5
Artichoke (globe)	1	8	1
Artichoke (Jerusalem)	1	8–16	4
Beans (runner)	2	6–10	15
Beans (broad)	1–2	6–10	20
Beans (round)	1	2	20
Beets (cylindrical)	4	3–6	15
Bok choi (pak choi)	3–4	4	5
Broccoli	2	6	5
Brussels sprouts	1	6–10	2
Bunching onions	1	6–12	20
Cabbage (round)	2	4	2–3
Cardoons	1	4–8	2
Carrots	3	9–11	50
Cauliflower	2	2	1
Celeriac	2	6	4
Celery	2	11	5
Celtuce	4	6	3–5
Chicory	3	2–3	5–10
Chinese broccoli (gai lohn)	6	2	6
Collards	2	8–16	5
Corn salad	8	1–2	10
Corn (sweet)	3	1	10–15
Corn (dried)	1	2	20–30
Courgettes	2	6–12	1
Cucumber	2	8	3
(Daikon) radish	4	5	6
Dandelion greens	6	1	6–8
Eggplant	1	10	3
Endive	3	6	6
Florence fennel	3	6	10
Garlic	2	4	1–3
Good King Henry	1	4	5

Vegetable	No. of added succession plantings in 8-month period	Harvest period (in weeks)	Plants per person for each planting
Hamburg parsley	2	6	8
Horseradish	1	12–15	1
Kale	2	6–15	5
Kohlrabi	2	2	6
Leeks	1	6–15	10–25
Lettuce	4	3–6	8
Melons	1	6–10	3
Mizuna	6	2	6
Mustard greens	3	6–12	5
New Zealand spinach	1	6–12	3
Okra	1	6–12	5
Onions	1	6	20
Parsnips	1	6–15	12
Peas (bush shell)	2	4–8	30–50
Peas (bush snap)	2	4–8	30–50
Peppers (sweet)	1	8–12	3
Peppers (hot)	1	8–12	1
Potatoes	2	2–3	5
Pumpkins	1	4–6	1
Purslane	3	3	5
Radicchio	1	5	10
Radish (round)	8	1–2	12
Salsify	1	6–15	12
Scallions	2	10–12	20–25
Scorzonera	1	6–12	4
Sea kale	1	3	5
Shallots	2	4–6	3
Spinach	4	3–6	10
Summer squash	2	6–12	1–2
Sunflower	1	2	2
Sweet potatoes	1	4–8	5
Swiss chard	2	6–20	3
Tomatoes	1	6–15	3
Turnips	4	2–4	3–5
Winter squash	1	2–4	2

Catch Cropping

Catch cropping is effectively the practice of following one crop with another in the same place. Usually, fast-growing and maturing vegetables are used to fill gaps between successive crops. Particular care must be taken with this system to ensure that follow-on crops are chosen in accordance with proper crop rotations. Intensive systems such as this can lead to rapid build-up of a pest or disease causing pathogen if not chosen properly.

Fast-Growing Crops Suitable for Intercropping and Catch Cropping

A few examples of vigorous-growing crops that may be sown in between rows of main crops:

Crop	Time to mature
Carrots	9 to 20 weeks
Endives	7 to 13 weeks
Lettuce	4 to 14 weeks
Radishes	4 to 8 weeks
Rocket (arugula)	3 to 5 weeks
Salad leaves	4 to 14 weeks
Spinach	5 to 10 weeks
Spring onions	8 to 10 weeks

Protected Cropping

Apart from growing plants under cover, such as greenhouses, frames and cloches, protection is required for those growing directly in the ground outside, especially from adverse climatic conditions. Winds can be very damaging to young plants as can early frosts but it is the combination of frost and wind that is the most damaging and more likely to kill them.

Only heated structures can provide frost-free protection but the use of various aids, such as plastic, fleece and low wattle fences, can all play an important part in providing some protection.

Advantages of using protective structures

- Extends the growing season both earlier and later in the year.
- Improves crops of half-hardy vegetables such as cucumbers and tomatoes.
- Better quality of many hardy winter vegetables than those grown outside.
- Provides an early start for plants that will be grown outdoors.
- Soil warms up more quickly, providing better conditions for good strong growth.

Strip Cropping

Strip cropping represents an effective way of using cloches and low poly-tunnels. The units are moved between two and three strips of land or beds so that they cover three or four crops at critical growing stages.

Square Spacing

This is for plants being grown in rows with the in-row spacing being the same as the between-row spacing. This layout is useful where only two or three plants can be placed across the bed.

SQUARE: in-row and between-row spacing are equal

Spacing and Vegetable Size

Spacing can now be used as a tool to determine the size of vegetable required. The larger the space the larger the vegetable will grow. Reduce the space for smaller vegetables, within reason.

For example: SUMMER CABBAGE
Small heads 35 x 35cm (14 x 14in)
Large heads 45 x 45cm (18 x 18in).

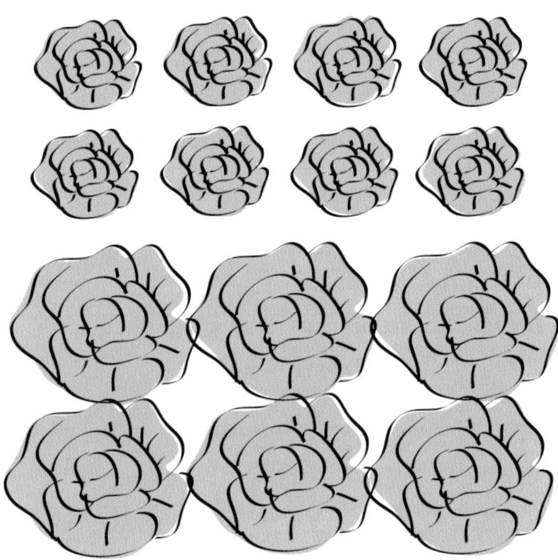

Reducing the spacing of crops such as cabbage will reduce the size of the crop

GROWING MEDIA

It is necessary to use a specific growing medium such as seed, cutting, potting or multi-purpose compost mix in order to grow healthy seedlings and plants in containers of various sizes and shapes.

The ideal growing medium

- *retains moisture and is well aerated;*
- *allows a vigorous root system to develop;*
- *includes the correct quantity of nutrients;*
- *has a uniform consistency;*
- *is free from any pathogens.*

Composts are available ready made or keen gardeners can make their own.

Self-made Compost

The main aim is to ensure the correct balance of bulk materials, nutrients, aeration and drainage to suit the selected plants and to conform to the above ideal.

The list below shows the ingredients that are suitable and the following chart, the 'recipes' for the three main mixtures.

INGREDIENTS

Composted bark

- Low-nutrient bulking agent.
- May suppress root diseases.
- Good buffering against high nutrient levels.
- Unsuitable for capillary matting systems.
- Too free-draining on its own, best mixed with other finer material.
- Unsuitable for small modules.

Coir

- Unsuitable for ericaceous plants.
- Adds bulk.
- High potassium content.
- Good aeration and water holding capacity.
- Encourages root growth.
- Surface dries out quickly whilst underneath remains moist – easy to overwater.
- Widely available.

Sawdust

- Good bulking agent when used in combination with loam for potting mixes.
- Very free-draining.
- Locks up nutrients.
- Needs thorough composting before use.

Recycled peat

- Harvested from watercourses.
- Similar to normal peat.
- Low-nutrient bulking agent.
- May not be weed free.

Leafmould (two years old)

- Low-nutrient bulking agent.
- Good moisture retention and consistency.

- Contains disease-combating micro-organisms.
- Makes a good seed-sowing medium on its own.
- May grow weed seedlings.
- Excellent addition to potting mixes, helps to maintain an open structure.

Grit or sand

- Washed sand, free of salt and other contaminants is best.
- Use coarse sand for loam-based growing media (particle sizes 0.2–2mm).
- Use fine sand for soilless mixes.

Perlite and vermiculite

- Lightweight materials to improve drainage.

Garden compost

- Adds bulk and nutrients.
- Best used in potting media.
- May help suppress diseases.
- May contain weed seeds.
- Batches may vary in quality and consistency.

Composted municipal green waste

- Adds bulk and some nutrients (high in potassium).
- Suppresses disease.
- Good buffering capacity.
- Unsuitable for ericaceous plants.
- Requires addition of inert material to balance nutrient status.

Mushroom compost

- Unsuitable for ericaceous plants.
- Adds bulk and nutrients.

Animal manures

- Not suitable for ericaceous plants.
- High nutrient content.
- Best composted with straw or other bulking agents.
- Useful for heavy feeders such as tomatoes.

Comfrey leafmould

- Nutrient-rich bulking agent, high in potassium.

Worm compost

- Ideal for plants requiring a rich mix.
- Good top dressing for pot plants.
- Holds large amounts of water, making it useful for inclusion in hanging baskets.

Loam

- Good-quality topsoil.

Limestone

- Used to raise pH.

Organic fertilizers

- Provide plant nutrients for potting mixes.

Acknowledgement: *Encyclopedia of Organic Gardening*

Plant raising and potting mixes

USE	Ingredients	Ratio (by vol)	Comments
SEED-SOWING MIXES	Leafmould alone		Often sufficient on its own if sieved
	Leafmould:loam	4:1	Gives good results with most seeds. Has enough nutrients until seedlings are transplanted; too coarse for small seeds. Needs careful watering
	Comfrey leafmould:sand	4:1	Will provide sufficient nutrients until potting-on stage
POTTING MIXTURES	Coir alone		Transplant seedlings promptly to avoid nutrient deficiencies
	Loam:leafmould:garden compost	1:1:1	A good basic mix, well-drained and fertile
	Peat substitute:sand:loam: garden compost	2:1:3:0.5	Nutrient rich
	Leafmould:worm-compost	3:1	Nutrient rich
	Loam:manure:leafmould	3:1:1	Very rich mix for heavy feeders such as pot-grown tomatoes and peppers
	Comfrey leafmould alone		Good for flowering and fruiting container-grown plants
	Comfrey leafmould:grit	4:1	To every 35 litres (8 gals) add 144g general organic fertilizer and 28g seaweed meal
	Leafmould:loam	1:1	Good for permanent plantings in pots. Loam does not require pasteurization. Use comfrey leafmould for a richer mix
	Loam:leafmould or coir	1:1	To every 35l (8gals), add 225g (8oz); 100g (4oz) bonemeal; 85g (3oz) hoof and horn; 55g (2oz) ground limestone. Nutrient rich
CUTTINGS MIXTURES	Coir:grit or perlite	1:1	
	Sieved leafmould:coarse sand	1:1	Use well-rotted leafmould

Vegetable growing guide

PLANT		SEASONAL			MEASUREMENTS					SOIL				CLIMATE		
NAME	ORDER	SOWING TIME	SITE	PLANTING TIME	SOWING DEPTH	SPACING BETWEEN PLANTS	SPACING BETWEEN ROWS	HEIGHT	SPREAD	NUTRITION	CULTURAL	pH	GERMINATION °C	PREFERRED	HARDINESS	LOCATION
ARTICHOKE Chinese	7		Direct	Spring (tubers)	40 - 75mm	300mm	450mm	Low	Narrow	General liquid feed in summer to stimulate growth	Rich soil, lots of organic matter, plenty of moisture, mulch heavily.	6.5 - 7.5		Warm to hot	Very Hardy	Full to moderate sun
ARTICHOKE Globe	3	February-March	Cover Direct	February-April (rooted suckers)	50mm	750 - 900mm	900mm	Medium	Medium	Nitrogen or liquid feed 6 weeks after planting	Dig deeply in winter, ensure good drainage and lots of compost or manure.	6.5 - 7.5		Warm to hot	Hardy Protect from full sun until established	Open not exposed-protected
ARTICHOKE Jerusalem	3		Direct	February-March (tubers)	130mm	300 - 400mm	Rows 900 - 1200mm	Very Tall	Medium	Moderate amounts of potassium and phospherous	Dig deeply in winter, ensure good drainage and lots of compost or manure.	6.5 - 7.5		Mainly cool	Very Hardy	Full sun
ASPARAGUS	4	February	Cover	Crowns March early April	100mm	300 - 450mm	300mm	Tall	Wide	Compost in autumn. Nitrogen or organic liquid feed	Apply plenty of compost and manure to a well drained soil.	6.3 - 7.5	13° - 16°	Open	Hardy	Full sun. Avoid exposed sites and frost pockets
ASPARAGUS Pea	8	Mid April to end May	Cover	May		250 - 300mm	380mm apart	Low	Narrow	High nitrogen	Medium to heavy soil dug and manured in autumn provides best results, apply compost.	6.0 - 7.0	13°	Warm	Tender	Full sun
AUBERGINE	12	Mid-March - mid-April	Cover	Late April-early May		400 - 450mm	900mm	Medium	Medium	High potash fertiliser every 10 -12 days once fruits start to set	Humus rich and good draining soil.	5.5 - 6.5	18°	Hot	Very Tender	Full sun sheltered
BEAN Broad	8	Nov - Jan March - May	Direct	-	50mm	150 - 200mm	600 - 900mm	Medium	Narrow	Soil slightly deficient in nitrogen	Ensure good soil preparation, only dig if ground is heavy.	5.5 - 6.7	Low	Any	Hardy	Full sun
BEAN French	8	March-April May - June	Cover Direct	Late May early June	40 - 50mm	150 - 250mm	300 - 350mm	Low	Narrow	Soil slightly deficient in nitrogen Potash	Dig in plenty of rotted manure, compost or organic matter during winter. Remedy any lime deficiency.	5.5 - 7.0	13°	Warm	Tender	Prefers full sun but can tolerate some shade. Shelter required
BEAN Runner	8	April May-June	Cover Direct	Late May	50mm	150 - 250mm	600mm	Climber	Narrow	Soil slightly defficient in nitrogen	Dig in plenty of rotted manure, compost or organic matter during winter. Remedy any lime deficiency.	5.5 - 7.0	10° - 12°	Warm, moist	Tender	Sheltered - full sun
BEETROOT	2	April - May	Direct	-	20mm	200 - 250mm	300mm	Low	Narrow	Seaweed	Apply compost in winter but no fresh manure.	6.5 - 7.0	8°	Any - cool	Hardy	Full sun
BROCCOLI Sprouting	4	March - May	Direct	June July	125mm	500 - 600mm	600 - 750mm	Medium	Medium	Ample nitrogen	Firm soil but not too rich. Follow peas or early potatoes.	6.5 - 7.0		Any - cool	Very Hardy	Full sun
BRUSSEL SPROUTS	4	February March - April	Cover Direct	May June	125mm	760mm	760mm	Medium	Medium	Ample nitrogen	Apply manure or compost in autumn (to allow soil to settle) before sowing.	6.5 - 7.0	8°	Any - cool	Very Hardy	Full sun protect from wind
CABBAGE Spring/Winter	4	July August	Cover	Mid-September	125mm	450mm	450mm	Medium	Medium	Nitrogen fertilizer or organic liquid - March - April	Apply manure or compost in autumn (to allow soil to settle) before sowing.	6.5 - 7.0	8°	Any - cool	Very Hardy	Full sun
CABBAGE Summer/Autumn	4	July August	Green house	Mid-September	125mm	450mm	450mm	Medium	Medium	Nitrogen fertilizer or organic liquid - March - April	Apply manure or compost in autumn (to allow soil to settle) before sowing.	6.5 - 7.0	8°	Any - cool	Very Hardy	Full sun
CALABRESE	4	Late March - early July	Direct	June - early July	125mm	450mm	600mm	Medium	Medium	Nitrogen/ liquid feed	Plenty of organic matter. Do not allow to dry out. Mulch heavily.	6.5 - 7.0	8°	Cold	Very Hardy	Full/partial shade
CARROTS	13	Early spring early summer	Direct		125-18mm	100mm	300mm	Low	Narrow	High potassium	Incorporate rotted leaves into soil in autumn. Use no fresh manure, ensure adequate water.	6.5 - 7.0	8°	Cool	Hardy	Sun sheltered
CAULIFLOWER Spring & Autumn	4	Jan - Feb March - April	Cover Direct	May - June	125mm	450 - 600mm	450 - 600mm	Medium	Medium	Low nitrogen	Plenty of organic matter, ensure adequate water. Do not over manure, soil must be well drained.	6.5 - 7.5	8°	Cool	Hardy	Full sun tolerates some shade
CELERIAC	13	Early March	Cover	May - June	05mm	300mm	400mm	Low	Narrow	Organic matter of High potassium	Quality depends on soil fertility and moisture. do not grow on thin chalk soil.	6.5 - 7.0	15° - 18°	Adequate moisture	Very Hardy	Full/partial sun
CELERY Green	13	Jan - Feb February	Cover Direct	May - June	05mm	230mm	230mm	Low	Narrow	Organic matter	Well manured and moist.	5.9 - 7.0	13°	Cool Moist	Tender	Full sun
COURGETTES	5	Feb - April May	Cover Direct	May - June	20mm	600-800mm	600mm	Medium	Very Wide	Organic matter	Prepare individual holes, using half organic matter or compost and half soil.	5.9 - 7.0	20°			
CUCUMBER Outdoor	5	April - May May	Cover Direct	May - June	10mm	450mm climbing 600 - 750mm flat	900mm	Medium	Wide	Seaweed	Dig deeply, ensuring good drainage take out holes and mix in compost forming a low mound.	6.5 - 7.0	18° - 20°	Warm moist	Tender	Full sun sheltered
ENDIVE	3	April - May May	Cover Direct	June - July August		250-300mm to 380mm		Low	Narrow	Some nitrogen	Plenty of organic matter, ensure adequate moisture.	neutral	13°	Cool moist	Tender	Full /partial sun
FENNEL Florence	12	May - July	Direct	August - Oct	10mm	150 - 200mm	450mm	Medium	Medium	Moderate nitrogen	Ensure fertile well drained soil with plenty of organic matter.	neutral	13°	Cool moist	Tender	Full sun
GARLIC	9			Feb - March	30mm	150mm	300mm	Low	V Narrow	Low requirement	Prefers light well drained soil.	6.0 - 7.0	10°	Cool	Hardy	Full/partial sun

Vegetable growing guide

PLANT		SEASONAL			MEASUREMENTS					SOIL				CLIMATE		
NAME	ORDER	SOWING TIME	SITE	PLANTING TIME	SOWING DEPTH	SPACING BETWEEN PLANTS	SPACING BETWEEN ROWS	HEIGHT	SPREAD	NUTRITION	CULTURAL	pH	GERMINATION °C	PREFERRED	HARDINESS	LOCATION
KALE	4	March - May	Direct	June - July	25mm	450mm	600 - 750mm	Medium	Medium	High nitrogen and Calcium	Succeeds on poor soil, but not waterlogged. Ensure adequate lime, use leaf mould.	6.5 - 7.0	10°	Cool	Very Hardy	Full/partial sun
KOHLRABI	4	February - August	Direct			150 - 230mm	200mm	Low	Narrow	High nitrogen	Apply leaf mould to soil.	5.5 - 6.7	10°	Cool	Hardy	Full/partial sun
LEEKS	9	Jan - Feb March - May	Cover Direct	May - July March	10mm	150 - 250mm	200mm	Low	V/Narrow	High nitrogen	Dig well in winter and apply organic matter.	6.0 - 6.5	10°	Cool	Very Hardy	Full/partial sun
LETTUCE	3	Jan - March March - Aug	Cover Direct	April - May	10mm	150 - 250mm	300 - 380mm	Low	Narrow	General fertilizer	Plenty of organic matter, ensure adequate moisture.	6.0 - 7.0	13°	Cool	Tender	Full/partial sun
MARROW Bush	5	Feb-April May	Cover Direct	May - June	30mm	600 - 900mm	600 - 900mm	Medium	V/Wide	Compost	Prepare individual holes, using half organic matter or compost and half soil.	5.9 - 7.0	20°	Warm Moist	Very Tender	Full sun
ONIONS	9	Dec - Feb	Direct Cover Direct	Spring (setts) Autumn April-May (setts)	10mm	150 - 250mm	300mm	Low	Narrow	Low nitrogen	Well cultivated and previously applied rotted manure. Firm with good tilth.	6.0 - 7.0	10°	Cool, open	Hardy	Full/partial sun
PARSLEY	13	March-July	Cover	May		150mm	250mm	Low	Narrow	Organic matter	Dig and manure site in winter. Ensure fine tilth for sowing in spring.	5.5 - 7.0	10°	Cool	Very Hardy	Full/partial sun
PARSNIP	13	April-May	Direct		30mm	250 - 300mm	450mm	Low	Narrow	None	Deep open well dug soil. No compost or manure. Leaf mould helps.	6.5	10°	Cool	Very Hardy	Full sun
PEAS	8	Earlies - early March 2nd earlies - early April Maincrop May	Direct		50 - 80mm	50 - 70mm	750 - 900mm	Vary	Narrow	None	Medium to heavy soil dug and manured in autumn provides best results. Apply compost.	6.5	7°	Cool - dislike intense heat	Tender	Full/partial sun
PEPPERS	12	Feb - March	Cover	June - July	10mm	600mm	450mm	Medium	Medium	Liquid feed fortnightly, high in potassium	Prepare ground in winter and enrich with compost or manure. Ensure good drainage.	5.5 - 7.0	18°	Warm	Very Tender	Full sun sheltered & protected
POTATOES	12		Direct	Earlies - mid March 2nd Earlies April Maincrop - May	100mm 380mm 380mm	Earlies - 300 - Maincrop -	380 - 500mm 760mm	Low Low Low	Wide Wide Wide	Nitrogen Nitrogen High Nitrogen	Dig in winter and ensure adequate humus. Use organic matter especially Comfrey in trench prior to planting.	5.6 - 6.0	-	Cool	Hardy	Full/partial sun No frost pockets
PUMPKIN	5	Feb - April May	Cover Direct	May - June	30mm	600 - 900mm	600 - 900mm	Medium	V/Wide	Compost	Prepare individual holes, using half organic matter or compost and half soil.	6.0 - 7.0	13°	Sunny	Very Tender	Full sun
RADISH	4	Spring autumn	Direct		10mm	25 - 50mm	300mm	Very Low	V/Narrow	Low nitrogen	Adequate compost and moisture.	6.0 - 6.5	8°	Cool	Hardy	Full/partial sun
SALISFY	3	March - May	Direct			150mm	600mm	Low	Narrow	High potassium	Deep, light stone free soil, manured from a previous crop.	6.5 - 7.0	13°	Cool	Hardy-protect with mulch	Full sun
SCORZONERA	3	Late spring			125mm	250mm	300mm	Low	Narrow	High potassium	Deep, light stone free soil, manured from a previous crop.	6.5 - 7.0	13°	Any	Hardy	Full/partial sun
SHALLOT	9	March	Direct	Setts - Spring and autumn	30mm	200mm	450mm	Low	Narrow	Low nitrogen	Well cultivated and previously applied rotted manure. Firm with good tilth.	6.0 - 7.0	10°	Any	Fairly Hardy	Full/partial sun
SEAKALE				Early - Late Spring		600 - 900mm	900mm	Medium	Medium	Seaweed	Prepare ground and ensure plenty of organic matter. Deep rich sandy soil best.	7.0	7 - 10°	Any	Resists light frosts, protect with mulch	Full sun
SPINACH/ SWISS CHARD	2	Spring & early autumn	Direct		30mm	150mm	300mm	Low	Narrow	High nitrogen	Apply compost, manure or organic matter and plenty of water druing growing period.	6.0 - 7.0	7°	Warm, moist	Tender	Full/partial sun
SPINACH NEW ZEALAND		Mid May - June			30mm	150mm	450mm	Medium	Wide	Fairly high nitrogen	Fertile, deeply cultivated well drained, plenty of compost, dry soils.	6.5 - 7.0	13°	Warm, moist	Very tender	Sunny
SQUASH	5	Spring			25mm	600 - 900mm	600 - 900mm	Very Wide	Narrow	Organic matter	Prepare individual holes, using half organic matter or compost and half soil.	6.0 - 7.0	13°	Warm, moist	Tender	Full sun
SWEDES	4	Early to late May	Direct			230mm	300mm	Narrow	Narrow	Nitrogen	Well dug soil, manured from a previous crop, no fresh manure.	5.5 - 7.0	10°	Warm, moist	Hardy	Full/partial sun
SWEET CORN	6	Late April Late May	Cover Direct	Late May - July	30mm	600mm	600mm	Tall	Medium	Basic dressing	Not too rich and containing no fresh manure. Dig in compost to conserve moisture.	5.5 - 6.5	13°	Warm	Tender	Full sun sheltered
TOMATOES	12	March - April	Cover	May - June	10mm	380 - 450mm	600 - 900mm	Medium	Medium	Basic dressing	Dig in winter, apply plenty of compost.	5.5 - 7.5	18°	Warm	Tender	Full sun sheltered
TURNIPS	4	April - July	Direct		10mm	100mm	250mm	Low	Narrow	High nitrogen	Any good soil not deficient in lime. No fresh manure.	5.5 - 7.0	15°	Cool, moist	Very hardy	Full/partial sun

LUNAR GARDENING

Description

Since time immemorial farmers and gardeners have held a belief that edible plants would benefit if they were planted in harmony with the phases and cycles of the Moon.

This practice has occurred in various guises and according to different traditions which have been passed down through the centuries.

In addition there are the basic cycles of the heavens to which birds, animals and the plants are very much attuned. Plants especially receive energy from the sun and are continually affected by the changing rhythm of the Moon.

Decisions on the most suitable time to sow, plant and harvest should take lunar cycles into account. This is especially relevant when the Moon is waxing and in the 48 hours before fullness, because crops sown at this time in all cases will grow better and faster.

Main principles

- Always plant when the Moon is waxing.
- The influence of the Moon is greatest when full.
- Never plant during a full moon eclipse.
- Try to plant or sow when the Moon is in a zodiac sign corresponding to the crop being sown.
- A bad aspect between Saturn and the Moon will damage a seed's effectiveness, and a good aspect will enhance it.

The moon month is made up of four quarters. These are referred to as the first, second, third and fourth quarter. In diaries they are referred to as 'new moon', 'first quarter', 'full moon' and 'last quarter'. See Diagram.

KEY

New Moon

First Quarter

Full Moon

Fourth Quarter

On the first day of the first quarter (new moon), the strength of the moon's gravitational pull upon Earth is at its weakest. The pull increases from that lowest point as the first quarter develops into and becomes the second quarter. At the end of the second quarter (full moon) and the start of the third, the gravitational pull is at its strongest.

When the third quarter begins, the strength of the pull starts to reduce. It goes on reducing through the third quarter and then through the fourth quarter. At the end of the fourth quarter, the gravitational pull is once again at its weakest.

This is when the moon is once again new and at the start of another first quarter.

The Earth's water table responds to this phenomenon. It rises as the strength of the moon's

Planting by the phases of the Moon

2 days before new moon

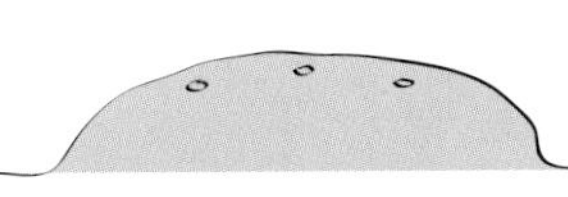

Plant short and extra long germinating seeds (most vegetables and herbs) into trays and/or beds

First 7 days

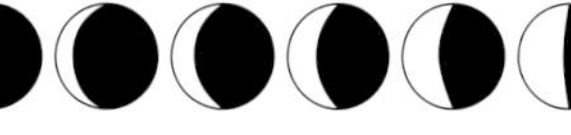

Balanced increase in rates of root and leaf growth

Moonlight +
Lunar activity –

Second 7 days

Increased leaf growth rate

Moonlight +
Lunar activity +

Full Moon

Transplant seedlings from trays into beds and plant long germinating seeds (most flowers) into trays and/or beds

Third 7 days

Increased root growth rate

Moonlight –
Lunar activity –

Fourth 7 days

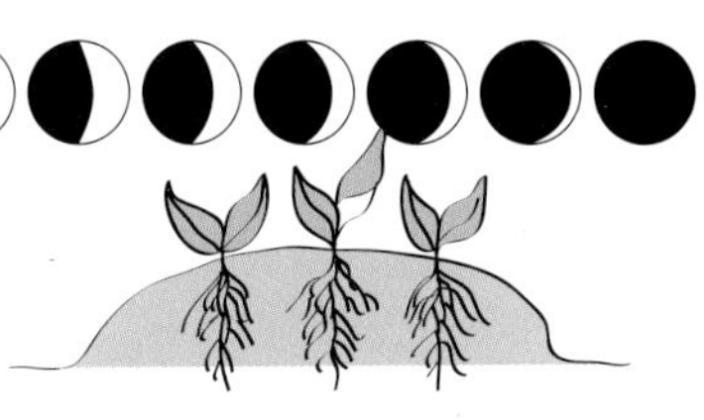

Balanced decrease in rate of root and leaf growth (resting period)

Moonlight –
Lunar activity –

gravitational pull increases, and falls back as the strength decreases.

As the water table rises, it exerts an upward pressure. This causes the moisture beneath the garden soil to rise. This, in turn, results in an increased moisture content at the level where gardeners do their gardening.

As the water table falls back, the pressure decreases and the topsoil's moisture content reduces.

This unfailing act of Nature – which is of greatest significance during summer's diminished rainfall and increased activity in the garden – can be of help to the aware gardener in a number of ways.

A bonus of moon gardening is that the amount of fertilizer applied at the correct moon time – at the start of and during the fourth quarter – can be reduced by as much as 50% of the manufacturer's recommended volume or weight.

During the moon's final phase, its pull on Earth diminishes to its weakest. In consequence, the water table beneath Earth's surface is permitted to slip back to its lowest level.

As the water table recedes, it draws to a deeper depth the fertilizer that is applied at the time. There is improved dispersal and, hence, there can be a reduction in the quantity used.

A consequent additional bonus is a reduction in the build-up of the chemicals that are now known to cause problems to both wild life and mankind. Every drop of run-off created by fertilizer application (and over-application, of which many gardeners are guilty) adds to that build-up.

Preparation

Begin the soil manoeuvring that is the essence of the fertilizing autumn dig at the start of the moon's fourth quarter. The fallen and still-falling water table releases pressure upon the dug soil and causes it to be at its most receptive to air and airborne higher temperatures. This combination encourages increased vegetable-processing activity by the creatures of the soil and thus enhances the process that results in increased fertility.

Feeding

Add manure and fertilizers to the soil at the start of the moon's fourth quarter – on the first day, ideally, or as close as possible to that time. The falling water table releases pressure upon the dug soil and encourages the more thorough and deeper absorption of additives.

POLLINATION

Bee-attracting plants

Many insects, including flies, pollinate plants, but the bee is the most important pollinator. It is attracted to plants because of their nectar, but it is the pollen, which accidentally attaches itself to the bee's body, that affects the pollination of plants.

Common name	Botanical name
Yarrow	*Achillea millefolium*
Bugle	*Ajuga reptans*
Chives	*Allium schoenoprasum*
Alkanet	*Anchusa azurea*
Dill	*Anethum graveolens*
Angelica	*Angelica archangelica*
Anthemis	*Anthemis*
Rockcress	*Arabis caucasica*
Michaelmas daisy	*Aster novi-belgii*
Bergenia	*Bergenia*
Borage	*Borago officinalis*
Butterfly bush	*Buddleia davidii*
Marigold	*Calendula*
Ling	*Calluna vulgaris*
Campanula	*Campanula*
Marsh marigold	*Caltha palustris*
Centaurea	*Centaurea*
Valerian	*Centranthus ruber*
Shasta daisy	*Chrysanthemum*

Common name	Botanical name
Convolvulus	*Convolvulus tricolor*
Tickweed	*Coreopsis grandiflora*
Cosmos	*Cosmos*
Cotoneaster	*Cotoneaster*
Crocus	*Crocus*
Delphinium	*Delphinium*
Foxglove	*Digitalis*
Teasel	*Dispasacus fullonum*
Globe flower	*Echinops ritro*
Heather	*Erica*
Sea Holly	*Eryngium*
Wallflowers	*Erysimum*
Californian poppy	*Eschscholzia californica*
Eucalyptus	*Eucalyptus*
Hemp agrimony	*Eupatorium*
Meadowsweet	*Filipendula ulmaria*
Fennel	*Foeniculum vulgare*
Cranesbill	*Geranium*
Baby's breath	*Gypsophila*

Bee-attracting plants continued

Common name	Botanical name
Ivy	*Hedera helix*
Sunflower	*Helianthus*
Cherry pie	*Heliotropium arborescens*
Hyssop	*Hyssopus officianlis*
Candytuft	*Iberis*
Dead nettle	*Laminium album*
Lavender	*Lavandula*
Mallow	*Lavatera*
Lovage	*Levisticum officinale*
Poached-egg plant	*Limnanthes douglasii*
Alyssum	*Lobularia maritime*
Honeysuckle	*Lonicera*
Honesty	*Lunaria biennis*
Yellow loosestrife	*Lysimachia punctata*
Balm	*Melissa officinalis*
Mint	*Mentha*
Bee balm	*Monarda didyma*
Grape hyacinth	*Muscari*
Forget-me-not	*Mysotis*
Sweet Cicely	*Myrrhis odorata*

Common name	Botanical name
Catmint	*Nepeta*
Marjoram	*Origanum vulgare*
Poppy	*Papaver officinale*
Phacelia	*Phacelia tanacetifolia*
Cherry	*Prunus*
Firethorn	*Pyracantha*
Mignonette	*Reseda odorata*
Flowering currant	*Ribes*
Rosemary	*Rosmarinus officinalis*
Blackberry	*Rubus*
Black Eyed Susan	*Rudbeckia*
Soapwort	*Saponaria officinalis*
Stonecrop	*Sedum*
Ice plant	*Sedum specatabile*
Goldenrod	*Solidago*
Comfrey	*Symphytum officinale*
Marigold	*Tagetes*
Thyme	*Thymus*
Clover	*Trifolium*

Larval food plants for butterflies and moths

Common name	Botanical name
Alder buckthorn	*Frangula alnus*
Bird's-foot trefoil	*Lotus corniculatus*
Common sorrel	*Rumex acetusa*
Cuckooflower	*Cardamine pratensis*
Dame's violet	*Hesperis matronalis*
Garlic mustard	*Alliaria petiolate*
Holly and	*Ilex aquifolium*
Ivy (for Holly Blue)	*Hedera helix*
Lime trees	*Tilia species*
Privet	*Ligustrum vulgare*
Stinging nettle	*Urtica dioica*
Various soft grasses	

Flowers for hoverflies and other beneficial insects

Common name	Botanical name
Blackthorn	*Prunus spinosa*
Brambles	*Rubus fruticosus*
Buckwheat	*Fagopyrum esculentum*
Californian poppy	*Eschscholzia californica*
Convolvulus annual	*Convolvulus tricolor*
Corn marigold	*Chrysanthemum segetum*
Cornflower	*Centaurea cyanus*
Coriander	*Coriandrum sativum*
Cow parsley	*Anthriscus sylvestris*
Dog rose	*Rosa canina*
Fennel	*Foeniculum vulgare*
Figwort	*Scrophularia*
Hawthorn	*Crataegus monogyna*
Ivy	*Hedera helix*
Phacelia	*Phacelia tanacetifolia*
Sweet alyssum	*Lobularia maritima*
Yarrow	*Achillea millefolium*

Flowers for adult butterflies

Common name	Botanical name
Aubretia	*Aubretia species*
Buddleia	*Especially B. x weyeriana and B. weyeriana 'Sugargold'*
Candytuft	*Iberis umbellata*
Hebe – particularly 'Great Orme' and 'Midsummer Beauty'	*Hebe species*
Field scabious	*Knautia arvensis*
Honesty	*Lunaria annua*
Hyssop	*Hyssopus officianlis*
Hemp agrimony	*Eupatorium cannabinum*
Ice plant	*Sedum spectabile*
Irish heath	*Erica erigena*
Ivy	*Hedera helix*
Lady's smock	*Cardamine pratensis*
Lavender ('Munstead' is one of the best)	*Lavendula*
Marjoram	*Origanum: wild forms are best*
Mint	*Mentha spp, especially applemint*
Michelmas daisy	*Especially Aster x frikartii 'Mönch'*
Small scabious	*Scabiosa columbaria*
Sweet rocket	*Hesperis matronalis*
Sweet William	*Dianthas barbatus*

Good nectar sources for insects

Common name	Botanical name
Applemint	*Mentha x rotundifolia*
Aubretia	*Aubretia species*
Blackthorn	*Prunus spinosa*
Bramble	*Rubus fructicosus*
Buddleia in various forms	*Buddleia davidii*
Convolvulus – Blue	*Caryopteris x clandonensis*
Ensign	*Convolvulus tricolor*
Dames's violet	*Hesperis matronalis*
Devil's bit scabious	*Succisa pratensis*
Fleabane	*Pulicaria dysenterica*
Globe thistle	*Echinops ritro*
Golden rods	*Solidago species*
Greater knapweed	*Centaurea scabiosa*
Hebe, various species	*Hebe albicans and Hebe brachysiphon*
Hemp agrimony	*Eupatorium cannabinum*
Honeysuckle	*Lonicera periclymenum and other species*
Hyssop	*Hyssopus officinalis*
Iceplant	*Sedum spectabile*
Lavender 'Dwarf Munstead Blue'	*Lavandula*
Marigolds, all sorts	*Tagetes*
Marjoram	*Origanum vulgare*
Michaelmas daisies Aster species, various	*Aster*
Night-scented stock	*Mathiola longipetala bicornis*
Red valerian	*Centranthus ruber*
Thyme	*Thymus drucei*
Tobacco plant	*Nicotiana species*
	Verbena venosa

Plants for beneficial insects and wildlife

Plant	Hover-flies	Bees	Lady-birds	Lace-wings	Butter-flies	Birds
Alkanet (*Anchusa azurea*)		✓				
Alyssum (*Lobularia maritime*)		✓			✓	
Angelica (*Angelica archangelica*)	✓					
Baby's breath (*Gypsophila*)		✓			✓	
Balm (*Melissa officinalis*)						
Borage (*Borago officinalis*)		✓				
Buddleia (*Buddleia davidii*)				✓	✓	
Bugle (*Ajugo reptans*)		✓				
Campanula species		✓				
Candytuft (*Iberis*)					✓	
Catmint (*Nepeta*)	✓				✓	
Centaurea	✓					
Cherry pie (*Heliotropium arborescens*)					✓	
Chives (*Allium schoenoprasum*)		✓				
Clover (*Trifolium*)	✓					
Comfrey (*Symphytum officinale*)		✓				
Convolvulus tricolour	✓			✓		
Cosmos	✓	✓		✓		
Cranesbill (*Geranium*)	✓					✓
Deadnettle (*Lamium album*)		✓				
Delphinium		✓				
Dill (*Anethum graveolens*)	✓					
Echinopsis ritro		✓				
Eschscholzia californica						
Fennel (*Foeniculum vulgare*)	✓	✓	✓			
Firethorn (*Pyracantha*)						✓
Flowering currant (*Ribes*)		✓				
Forget-me-not (*Myosotis*)		✓				
Foxglove (*Digitalis*)		✓				

Plants for beneficial insects and wildlife continued

Plant	Hover-flies	Bees	Lady-birds	Lace-wings	Butter-flies	Birds
Goldenrod (*Solidago*)	✓	✓		✓		
Grape hyacinth (*Muscari*)		✓				
Honesty (*Lunaria biennis*)					✓	✓
Honeysuckle (*Lonicera*)		✓			✓	
Hyssop (*Hyssopus officinalis*)		✓				
Ice plant (*Sedum spectabile*)		✓			✓	
Lavender (*Lavandula*)		✓				
Lovage (*Levisticum officinale*)	✓					
Mallow (*Lavatera*)		✓				
Marigold (*Calendula*)	✓		✓			
Marigold (*Tagetes*)	✓					
Marjoram (*Origanum vulgare*)		✓			✓	
Meadowsweet (*Filipendula ulmaria*)						✓
Mignonette (*Reseda odorata*)		✓			✓	
Mint (*Mentha*)	✓				✓	
Phacelio tanacetifolia	✓	✓				
Poached-egg plant (*Limnanthes douglasii*)	✓	✓				
Poppy (*Papaver officinale*)		✓				
Rockcress (*Arabis caucasico*)		✓				
Rosemary (*Rosmarinus officinalis*)		✓				
Sea holly (*Eryngium*)		✓				
Shasta daisy (*Chrysanthemum*)	✓					
Soapwort (*Saponaria officinalis*)					✓	
Sunflower (*Helianthus*)		✓			✓	✓
Teasel (*Dipsocus fullonum*)		✓			✓	✓
Thyme (*Thymus*)		✓				
Tickweed (*Coreopsis grandiflora*)		✓				
Valerian (*Centranthus ruber*)					✓	
Wallflowers (*Erysimum*)		✓				
Yarrow (*Achillea millefolium*)	✓	✓	✓	✓		
Yellow loosestrife (*Lysimachia punctata*)		✓				

Food plants for birds

Common Name	Botanical Name	FEATURES		Period
		Berries	Birds	
Barberry	*Berberris thunbergii*	Bright red berries	Thrushes, including fieldfares and redwings	Winter
Cotoneaster	*Cotoneaster horizontalis*	Red berries	Thrushes of all kinds and redwings including starlings, finches, crows, blue tits, thrushes and waxwings	Winter
Common hawthorn	*Crataegus monogymna*	Dark red berries	Thrushes of all kinds and redwings including starlings, finches, crows, blue tits, thrushes and waxwings	Winter
Ivy	*Hedera helix*	Berries	Wood pigeons, collared doves, waxwings, thrushes, jays, starlings and finches	Autumn and winter
Common holly	*Ilex acquifolium*	Red berries	Mistle thrushes	Autumn and winter
Himalayan honeysuckle	*Leycesteria formosa*	Red-purple berries	Tits, thrushes, finches and warblers	Autumn
Honeysuckle	*Lonicera periclymenum*	Glossy red berries	Robins, blackbirds, song thrushes, garden warblers, tits, crows, finches and waxwings	Autumn
Pyracantha	*Pyracantha* 'Orange Glow'	Vivid orange fruits	Wood pigeons and thrushes	Autumn to winter
Red-berried elder	*Sambucus racemosa*	Red berries	Waxwings and thrushes	Autumn
Whitebeam	*Sorbus aria*	Colourful berries	Wood pigeons, fieldfares, redwings, blackbirds and mistle thrushes	Autumn

WATERING

Water is essential for the success of organic edible gardening and needs to be conserved at all times. The soil is the plant's reservoir of water and, as soils differ in their make-up, some hold water better than others. For example, light sandy soils have the poorest water-holding capacity whereas the silty loams have the best retentive qualities.

Water loss

Water in the soil is lost through evaporation, which is affected by sunshine, temperature, wind, humidity, and the amount of existing moisture in the soil. Evaporation is greatest from a moist surface in dry, sunny, windy weather. Once the top 3cm (1in) of soil has dried out, evaporation is reduced.

Ways to conserve water

- Improve the soil structure by the application of compost.
- Mulch the soil to prevent evaporation.
- Dig the soil every so often to encourage roots to grow deeper.
- Do not cultivate soil in dry weather.
- Remove weeds, especially as seedlings, as quickly as possible.
- Consider spacing of plants according to their final size.
- Provide shelter from winds to all crops.
- Consider an irrigation system with sensors and automatic controls for the edible garden, instead of hand watering, which can be wasteful and ineffective.
- Collect rainwater from building roofs in tanks or containers. Rainwater is better than tap water as it does not contain any artificial chemicals.
- Do not water during the heat of the day.
- Improve drainage.
- Reduce plant density.
- Provide shelter on exposed sites.

It is important to consider the water requirements of the plants at the various stages of their development to ensure their success. Many plants go through a moisture-sensitive period when the supply of water to them is crucial. A moisture meter is a useful appliance to have for checking the soil.

Water-conserving methods

Together the five techniques described below conserve moisture far more effectively and more certainly than any single technique, and the benefits extend far beyond water conservation.

Method	Benefits
High organic matter content	holds moisture adds fertility stores nutrients boosts soil life fluffs soil
Deep mulching	slows evaporation cools soil adds fertility boosts soil life smothers weeds
Water-conserving plants	need less water survive drought
Dense plantings	shade soil smother weeds
Soil contouring	catches water directs water where needed helps plants and soil life survive both wet and dry periods builds humus adds visual interest

Effective watering

- As a rough guide, all plants need sufficient water when young until their roots are established.
- Vegetables grown for their leaves should never be allowed to dry out.
- Fast-growing plants, such as courgettes and marrows, need plenty of water right through their short growing season.
- Overwatering can produce a lot of soft growth attractive to pests, and make plants susceptible to cold or rotting off.
- Edibles grown for their roots, pods and fruits need steady but not excessive water until the flowers, fruits or roots start to form.
- Potatoes profit from a good dousing when the tubers are the size of marbles.
- When watering, make it thorough – at least 11 litres per sq m or 2 gallons per sq yd. The water should soak to the lower depths of the soil to encourage the roots to grow down. If water is just sprinkled, the roots will look no further and can dry out very quickly.
- Water brassicas at the base to avoid the damp conditions on the leaves that can encourage fungal disease.
- For plants sensitive to cold (such as tomatoes and aubergines), use water from the water butt.
- Adapt 'point watering' – directing the water to the base of the plant and leaving the surrounding area dry or, better still, mulched.
- Be gentle – water lightly on plants and soil.

Effective watering

- Water in the early morning.
- Apply water directly to soil, not plants.
- Water at critical growth stages.
- Use a soaker hose rather than a sprinkler.
- Use a timer to control supply.

Watering seeds

The best policy is to dribble water into the seed drill before planting, 1 litre to 1.30m (1 gallon to 20ft). Use a light rose, directing spray upwards so that smaller droplets are produced.

Watering transplants

Transplants are particularly vulnerable and need nursing until they establish. Water before and after transplanting, water little and often. In dry weather use 140ml (1/4 pint) for each plant.

Excess watering

- Wastes water.
- Dilutes nutrients.
- Damages soil structure.
- Overhead watering causes 'capping' or soil crust.
- Encourages shallow rooting, with plants becoming even more susceptible to water shortages.
- Root diseases can become more common.
- Flavour of crops, especially fruit, can be affected.
- Slugs and snails will be more prevalent.

Watering transplants

Least Thirsty Vegetables	Thirsty Vegetables
Beetroot	IN FLOWER
Broccoli – sprouting	Beans
Brussels sprouts	Peas
Cabbage – spring & winter	Potatoes
Carrots	Sweetcorn
Cauliflower – winter	IN FRUIT
Leek	Beans
Swede	Courgettes
Turnip	Marrows
	Peas
	Sweetcorn
	Tomatoes
	CONTINUOUS
	All leaf vegetables
	Cabbage – summer

Leaf Crops

Water frequently for heavy yields. In dry months use 11–16 litres per square metre (2–3 gallons per square yard) per week. When shortages occur use 22 litres per square metre (4 gallons per square yard) from 10–20 days before crops mature.

Fruit Crops

Vegetables that offer edible seeds and fruit have a critical watering period at flowering time and when fruits are setting and swelling. Use 22 litres per square metre (4 gallons per square yard) per week.

Critical watering times for vegetables

CROP	WHEN TO WATER	EFFECT
Artichoke (Jerusalem)	Never	Water would lower yield
Bean (broad)	When in flower	Increases crop
Bean (French)	Water only to help germination	Watering can lower yields
Bean (runner)	Before sowing, then at least weekly; in very hot weather daily	Much bigger yields
Beetroot	Water to help germination	
Brussels sprout	Puddle plants in if soil is dry	
Cabbage (Chinese)	Water daily in dry weather	Without regular water, plants go to seed
Cabbage (spring)	Puddle plants in if soil is dry	
Cabbage (summer)	Puddle plants in, water regularly in drought	Increased yield prevents plants going to seed
Calabrese	Water every 2–3 days in drought	Maintains yield
Carrot	Water only to help germination	Watering at any other time lowers yield
Cauliflower (summer)	Puddle in; never allow to go short of water	Any shortage of water will cause plant to go to seed
Celery	Water daily	Any lack of water could cause the crop to fail completely
Courgette	Water only when fruits start to swell, unless weather is very dry	Watering at other times encourages leaf formation
Cucumber (ridge)	Water as often as you can	Gives better texture and increased yield

6 THE PROTECTION

- Companion Planting
- Biological Controls
- Plant Pest Controls
- Host and Decoy Plants
- Plant Pests
- Traps, Barriers and Deterrents
- Organic Controls
- Mulching
- Weed Management

Companion Planting Chart

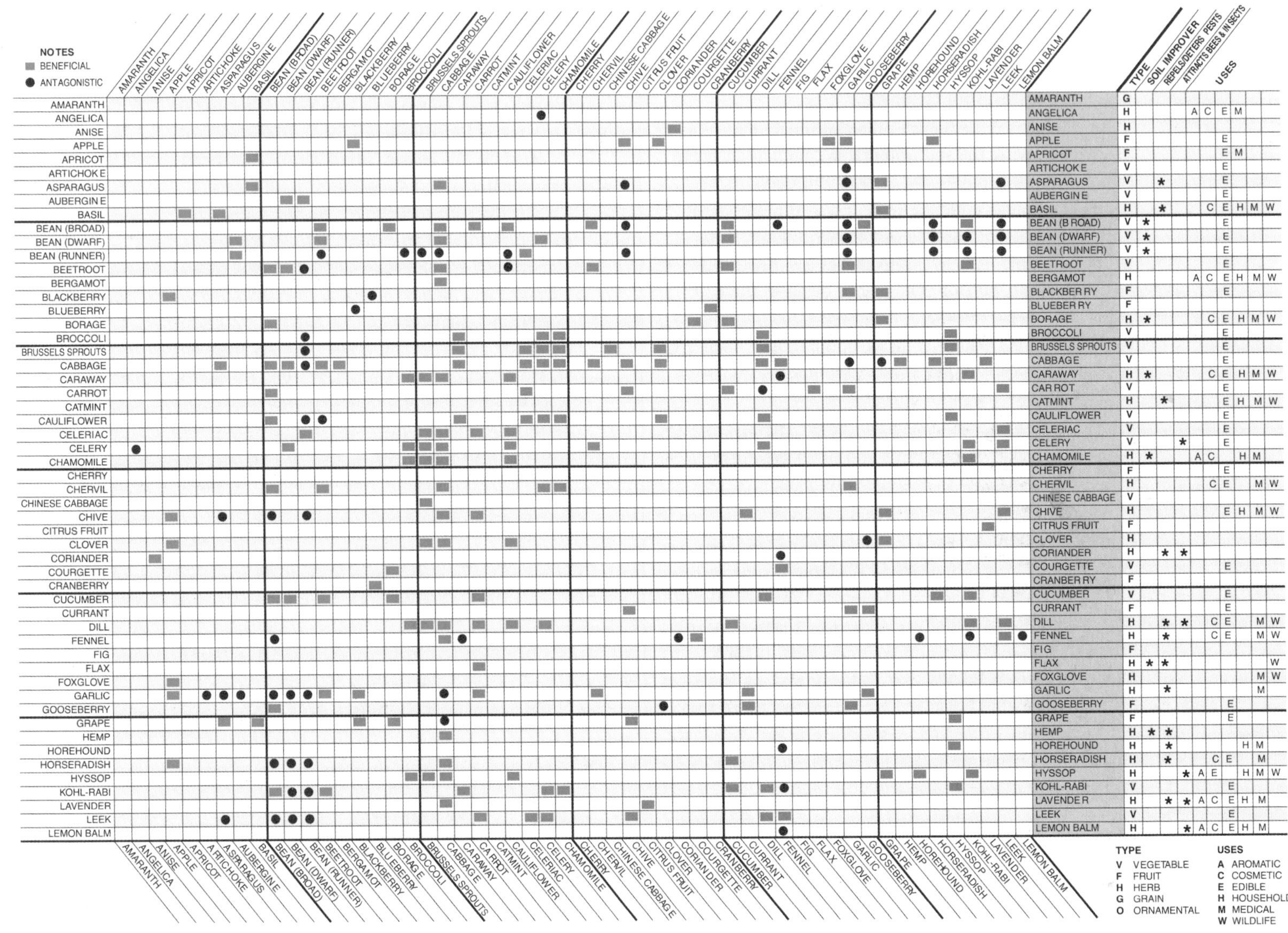

Plant	Type	Soil improver	Repels/deters pests	Attracts bees & insects	Uses
AMARANTH	G				
ANGELICA	H				A C E M
ANISE	H				
APPLE	F				E
APRICOT	F				E M
ARTICHOKE	V				E
ASPARAGUS	V		*		E
AUBERGINE	V				E
BASIL	H		*		C E H M W
BEAN (BROAD)	V	*			E
BEAN (DWARF)	V	*			E
BEAN (RUNNER)	V	*			E
BEETROOT	V				E
BERGAMOT	H				A C E H M W
BLACKBERRY	F				E
BLUEBERRY	F				
BORAGE	H	*			C E H M W
BROCCOLI	V				E
BRUSSELS SPROUTS	V				E
CABBAGE	V				E
CARAWAY	H	*			C E H M W
CARROT	V				E
CATMINT	H		*		E H M W
CAULIFLOWER	V				E
CELERIAC	V				E
CELERY	V			*	E
CHAMOMILE	H	*			A C H M
CHERRY	F				E
CHERVIL	H				C E M W
CHINESE CABBAGE	V				
CHIVE	H				E H M W
CITRUS FRUIT	F				
CLOVER	H				
CORIANDER	H		*	*	
COURGETTE	V				E
CRANBERRY	F				
CUCUMBER	V				E
CURRANT	F				E
DILL	H		*	*	C E M W
FENNEL	H		*		C E M W
FIG	F				
FLAX	H	*	*		W
FOXGLOVE	H				M W
GARLIC	H		*		M
GOOSEBERRY	F				E
GRAPE	F				E
HEMP	H	*	*		
HOREHOUND	H		*		H M
HORSERADISH	H		*		C E M
HYSSOP	H			*	A E H M W
KOHL-RABI	V				E
LAVENDER	H		*	*	A C E H M
LEEK	V				E
LEMON BALM	H			*	A C E H M

NOTES

■ BENEFICIAL

● ANTAGONISTIC

Plant	Amaranth	Angelica	Anise	Apple	Apricot	Artichoke	Asparagus	Aubergine	Basil	Bean (Broad)	Bean (Dwarf)	Bean (Runner)	Beetroot	Bergamot	Blackberry	Blueberry	Borage	Broccoli	Brussels Sprouts	Cabbage	Caraway	Carrot	Catmint	Cauliflower	Celeriac	Celery	Chamomile
LETTUCE													■					●				■				■	
LOVAGE																										●	
MARIGOLD							■		■	■	■	■															
MARJORAM										■	■	■						■		■							
MARROW																	■										
MELON																											
MINT				■										■				■	■	■				■			■
MORNING GLORY																											
MULBERRY																											
NASTURTIUM				■	■					●		●								■							
NECTARINE							■																				
ONION	■						●	●		●	●	●	■							■		■			■		■
OATS					●					■																	
OKRA								●		●	●	●															
OREGANO																			■	■							
PARSLEY		■				■	■		■					■													
PARSNIP																											
PEACH							■																				
PEAR																											
PEA								■		■	■	■										■					■
PENNY ROYAL																		■	■	■							
PEPPERS									■													■					
PLUM																											
POTATO	■			●	●			■		■	■							■	■	■				■		■	■
PUMPKIN																											
QUINCE																											
RADISH																			●	●		■	■	●			
RASPBERRY															●	●											
RHUBARB																											
ROSEMARY										■	■	■						■	■	■		■		■			
ROSE																											
RUE									●																		●
SAGE																		■	■	■		■		■			
SALSIFY																						■					
SCORZONERA																						■					
SOUTHERNWOOD				■	■													■	■	■			■	■			
SOYA BEAN											■																
SPINACH										■								●	●	●				●			
SQUASH											■						■										
STRAWBERRY											■	■					■	●	●	●				●			
SUMMER SAVORY									■	■	■	■															
SUNFLOWER													●					●	●	●							
SWEDE												●											■				
SWEETCORN	■									■	■	■							■								
SWEET PEPPER								■																			
TANSY				■	■				●						■												
TARRAGON								■																			
THYME								■		■	■							■	■	■			■	■			
TOMATO					●		■		■		■						■	●	●	●	●	■		●	■	■	
TURNIP																							■				
VALERIAN																											
WINTER SAVORY										■	■	■															
WORMWOOD			●						●									■	■	■	●	■		■			
YARROW																											

Plant	Cherry	Chervil	Chinese Cabbage	Chive	Citrus Fruit	Clover	Coriander	Courgette	Cranberry	Cucumber	Currant	Dill	Fennel	Fig	Flax	Foxglove	Garlic	Gooseberry	Grape	Hemp	Horehound	Horseradish	Hyssop	Kohl-Rabi	Lavender	Leek	Lemon Balm	Type	Soil Improver	Repels/Deters Pests	Attracts Bees & Insects	Uses
LETTUCE		■								■			●		■		■								●			V				E
LOVAGE										■																		H				E M W
MARIGOLD					■					■																		H		★		C E H M W
MARJORAM				●						●							●								■	●		H		★		
MARROW													■															V				E
MELON																												F				
MINT																								■				H		★		A C E H M
MORNING GLORY																																
MULBERRY																			■									F				E
NASTURTIUM								■		■																		H		★		E M W
NECTARINE																			■									F				
ONION		■										■												■		■		V				E W
OATS																												G	★			E
OKRA																	■											V				E
OREGANO										■																		H				E W
PARSLEY																									●			H			★	C E H M W
PARSNIP																												V		★	★	
PEACH				■													■		■									F				E
PEAR						■				■	■						■											F				E
PEA				●						■							●					●				●		V	★			E
PENNY ROYAL																												H		★		
PEPPERS													●											●				V				E
PLUM	●	●									■						■											F				E
POTATO								●		●					■	■				■		■		■	■		■	V				E
PUMPKIN																												V				E
QUINCE																	■											F				
RADISH		■		■			■			■		■							●				●					V		★		E
RASPBERRY																	■											F				E
RHUBARB																	■											F				E
ROSEMARY								●		●														■				H		★	★	A C E H M W
ROSE				■													■											H				A C E M
RUE		●						●						■							■				●		●	H		★		C E M
SAGE								●		●									■					■				H		★		C E H M
SALSIFY																										■		V		★		E
SCORZONERA																																
SOUTHERNWOOD											■													■				H		★		H M
SOYA BEAN				●													●									●		V	★		★	E
SPINACH							■					■										■		●				V				E
SQUASH													■															V				E
STRAWBERRY																	●							●		■		F				E
SUMMER SAVORY																												H		★	★	A W
SUNFLOWER										■																		H	★		★	C E H M
SWEDE																												V				E
SWEETCORN			■					■		■		■																V				E
SWEET PEPPER																								●				V				E
TANSY					■			■		■								■	■									H		★	★	C E H M W
TARRAGON													●															H				E M
THYME								●		●														■	■			H		★		A C E H M W
TOMATO				■								■	●			■		■				■		●			■	V				E
TURNIP													●															V				E
VALERIAN																												H	★			C E H M W
WINTER SAVORY																												H		★	★	C E H M
WORMWOOD					■								●											■				H		★		H M
YARROW																												H		★	★	H M W

TYPE

V VEGETABLE
F FRUIT
H HERB
G GRAIN
O ORNAMENTAL

USES

A AROMATIC
C COSMETIC
E EDIBLE
H HOUSEHOLD
M MEDICAL
W WILDLIFE

Companion Planting Chart continued

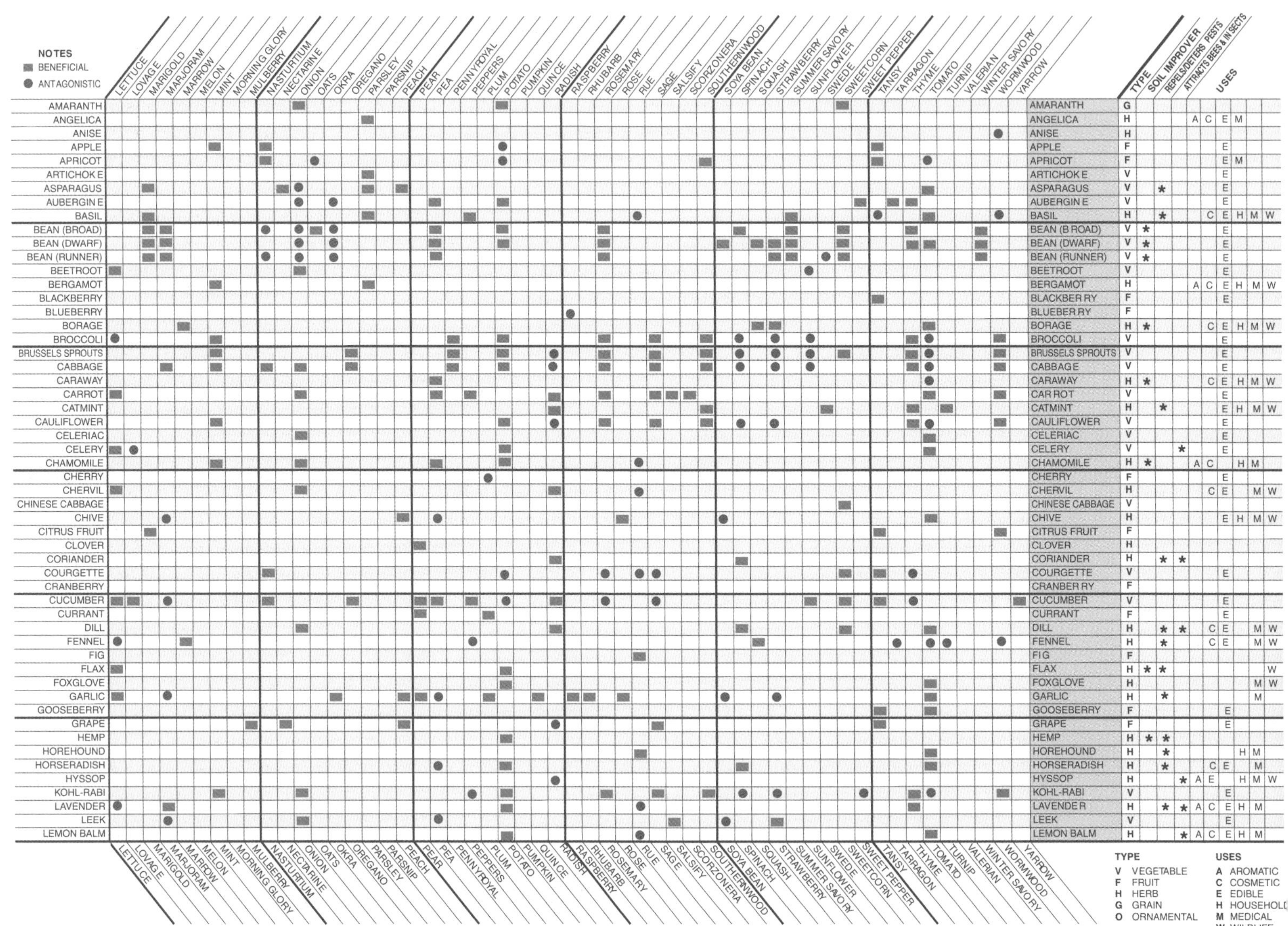

Plant	Type	Soil improver	Repels/deters pests	Attracts bees & insects	Uses
AMARANTH	G				
ANGELICA	H				A C E M
ANISE	H				
APPLE	F				E
APRICOT	F				E M
ARTICHOKE	V				E
ASPARAGUS	V		*		E
AUBERGINE	V				E
BASIL	H		*		C E H M W
BEAN (BROAD)	V	*			E
BEAN (DWARF)	V	*			E
BEAN (RUNNER)	V	*			E
BEETROOT	V				E
BERGAMOT	H				A C E H M W
BLACKBERRY	F				E
BLUEBERRY	F				
BORAGE	H	*			C E H M W
BROCCOLI	V				E
BRUSSELS SPROUTS	V				E
CABBAGE	V				E
CARAWAY	H	*			C E H M W
CARROT	V				E
CATMINT	H		*		E H M W
CAULIFLOWER	V				E
CELERIAC	V				E
CELERY	V			*	E
CHAMOMILE	H	*			A C H M
CHERRY	F				E
CHERVIL	H				C E M W
CHINESE CABBAGE	V				
CHIVE	H				E H M W
CITRUS FRUIT	F				
CLOVER	H				
CORIANDER	H		*	*	
COURGETTE	V				E
CRANBERRY	F				
CUCUMBER	V				E
CURRANT	F				E
DILL	H		*	*	C E M W
FENNEL	H		*		C E M W
FIG	F				
FLAX	H	*	*		W
FOXGLOVE	H				M W
GARLIC	H		*		M
GOOSEBERRY	F				E
GRAPE	F				E
HEMP	H	*	*		
HOREHOUND	H		*		H M
HORSERADISH	H		*		C E M
HYSSOP	H			*	A E H M W
KOHL-RABI	V				E
LAVENDER	H		*	*	A C E H M
LEEK	V				E
LEMON BALM	H			*	A C E H M

TYPE
V VEGETABLE
F FRUIT
H HERB
G GRAIN
O ORNAMENTAL

USES
A AROMATIC
C COSMETIC
E EDIBLE
H HOUSEHOLD
M MEDICAL
W WILDLIFE

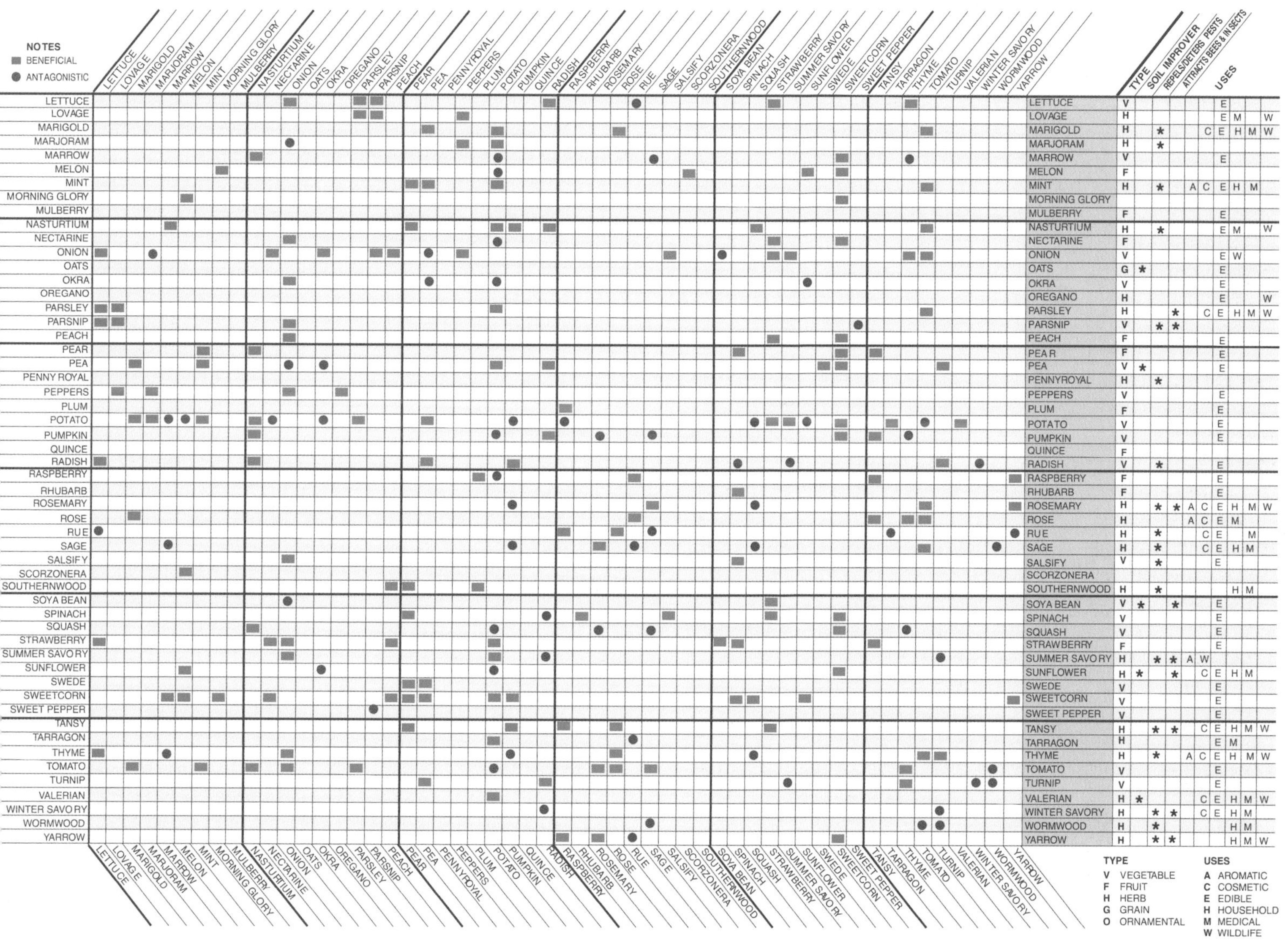

Plant	Type	Soil improver	Repels/deters pests	Attracts bees & insects	Uses
LETTUCE	V				E
LOVAGE	H				E M W
MARIGOLD	H		*		C E H M W
MARJORAM	H		*		
MARROW	V				E
MELON	F				
MINT	H		*		A C E H M
MORNING GLORY					
MULBERRY	F				E
NASTURTIUM	H		*		E M W
NECTARINE	F				
ONION	V				E W
OATS	G	*			E
OKRA	V				E
OREGANO	H				E W
PARSLEY	H			*	C E H M W
PARSNIP	V		*	*	
PEACH	F				E
PEAR	F				E
PEA	V	*			E
PENNYROYAL	H		*		
PEPPERS	V				E
PLUM	F				E
POTATO	V				E
PUMPKIN	V				E
QUINCE	F				
RADISH	V		*		E
RASPBERRY	F				E
RHUBARB	F				E
ROSEMARY	H		*	*	A C E H M W
ROSE	H				A C E M
RUE	H		*		C E M
SAGE	H		*		C E H M
SALSIFY	V		*		E
SCORZONERA					
SOUTHERNWOOD	H		*		H M
SOYA BEAN	V	*		*	E
SPINACH	V				E
SQUASH	V				E
STRAWBERRY	F				E
SUMMER SAVORY	H		*	*	A W
SUNFLOWER	H	*		*	C E H M
SWEDE	V				E
SWEETCORN	V				E
SWEET PEPPER	V				E
TANSY	H		*	*	C E H M W
TARRAGON	H				E M
THYME	H		*		A C E H M W
TOMATO	V				E
TURNIP	V				E
VALERIAN	H	*			C E H M W
WINTER SAVORY	H		*	*	C E H M
WORMWOOD	H		*		H M
YARROW	H		*	*	H M W

TYPE
- **V** VEGETABLE
- **F** FRUIT
- **H** HERB
- **G** GRAIN
- **O** ORNAMENTAL

USES
- **A** AROMATIC
- **C** COSMETIC
- **E** EDIBLE
- **H** HOUSEHOLD
- **M** MEDICAL
- **W** WILDLIFE

BIOLOGICAL CONTROLS

Many commercial growers use biological controls in greenhouses and these are now available to the home gardener. Most are widely employed for the control of whiteflies, red spider mites, aphids and mealy bugs in the greenhouse, where there is often an absence of natural predators.

The application of biological controls in the greenhouse or garden involves using predatory insects or other beneficial animals to control commonly occurring pests. Many pests are only a problem because their natural predators are missing from the garden. Introducing a biological control usually results in rapid control of the pest.

Biological controls

NAME	PREFERRED TEMPERATURE RANGE	WHAT THEY CONTROL
Amblyseus cucmreis (predatory mite)	25°C (77°F) 21°C (70°F); needs 80%+ humidity	The nymphal forms and adults consume large quantities of immature thrips.
Aphidoletes aphidimyza (predatory midge larva)		Tiny mosquito-like midge larvae that control substantial populations of more than 60 species of aphids.
Cryptolaemus montrouzieri (predatory beetle)	20-25°C (68-77°F)	This ladybird is effective in controlling mealy bugs on household plants and in greenhouses.
Encarsia Formosa (parasitic nematode	18-25°C (68-77°F)	Minute, flying parasitic wasps, which lay their eggs inside whitefly scales (the pupa stage) and eat them in two to four weeks.
Heterorhabditis megidis (parasitic nematode)	Minimum soil temperature of 14°C (57°F). If temperature drops below 20°C (68°F), they become less effective.	Patrol the soil to a depth of about 18cm (7in) and quickly take care of the slow-moving grubs, like vine weevil grubs and chafers. Very effective in pots and containers. Soil must be moist.
Metaphycus helvolus (parasitic wasp)	20-30°C (68-86°F)	These tiny, black and yellow wasps are effective against several soft-scale species, including brown scale. The females lay their eggs under the body of first- and-second-stage scales. The grubs feed on scales and develop into adults within two weeks. Adults also provide control by feeding on non-parasitized scales. *Metaphycus* are most effective in semi-tropical conditions.
Phasmarhabditis hermaphrodita (parasitic nematode)	Minimum soil temperature of 5°C (40°F)	Useful for slug control. Should be applied during early growing stages of vulnerable plants. Needs moist soil.
Phytoseiulus persimilis (predatory mite)	Use once temperature is regularly above 15°(60°F). Best at 18-25°C (64-77°F); needs 60%+ humidity	Predator mites, slightly larger than the two-spotted mites (also known as red spider mites) upon which they feed.
Steinemema feltiae (parasitic nematode)	Minimum temperature of 10°C (50°F), although they remain effective when the soil temperature drops below this.	Aggressive predators used to control fungus gnats, mushroom flies and leatherjackets. They can be used on lawns as well as in flower and vegetable gardens, fields, orchards and greenhouses.

PLANT PEST CONTROLS

Many insect species that feed on crop pests such as aphids, whiteflies etc. as juveniles (or larvae) feed on nectar and pollen as adults. Therefore maintaining a diverse flowering flora attracts adults of these species to the garden where they seek-out pest infestations and lay their eggs on them.

The following are those plants that have been shown to attract adults of beneficial 'pest-controllers' to the garden. It is not exhaustive but gives a guide on what can be planted to encourage them. Always plant some in and around the vegetable garden of the allotment.

However, hygiene is also important, such as keeping plants in good condition, free from weeds that could harbour any pests. Greenhouses and cold frames especially need to be kept clean and tidy at all times.

Pest controllers

COMMON NAME	BOTANICAL NAME	TYPE	CONTROLS
African marigold	*Tagetes erecta*	F	Reduces nematodes
Anise	*Pimpinella anisum*	F	Deters aphids, fleas, reduces cabbage worms
Alfafa, or lucerne	*Medicago sativa*		Reduces corn worms
Basil	*Ocimum basilicum*	H	Aphids, asparagus beetles
Bean	*Phaseolus*	V	Reduces corn armyworms
Black nightshade	*Solanum nigrum*	F	Reduces Colorado beetles
Borage	*Borage officinalis*	H	Attracts bees, reduces Japanese beetle on potatoes, and deters tomato hornworms
Broccoli	*Brassica oleacea*	V	Reduces striped cucumber beetles
Caper spurge	*Euphorbia lathyrus*	V	Deters moles
Carrot	*Daucus carota*	V	Deters onion flies
Castor bean	*Ricinus communis*	V	Controls moles, mosquitoes, and nematodes
Catnip	*Nepeta cataria*	H	Deters ants, aphids, Colorado beetles, darkling beetles, flea beetles, Japanese beetles, squash bugs, weevils
Celery	*Apium graveolens*	V	Deters cabbage butterflies
Chestnut	*Castanea sativa*		Beet moths
Chives	*Allium schoenoprasum*	H	Apple scab, mildew on cucumbers, gooseberries, summer squash and pumpkins
Chrysanthemum	*Chrysanthemum coccineum*	F	Reduces nematodes
Citrus fruit	*Citrus*	T	Autumn armyworms and ballworms
Clover	*Trifolium*	F	Deters cabbage root flies
Coriander	*Coriandrum sativum*	H	Aphids, spider mites, Colorado beetle
Corn	*Zea mays*	V	Reduces striped cucumber beetle
Dandelion	*Taraxacum officinale*	H	Repels Colorado beetles
Dead nettle	*Lamium album*	H	Deters potato bugs
Dill	*Anethum graveolens*	H	Deters aphids and spider mites

Type: F = Flower H = Herb V = Vegetable T = Tree Source: *Companion Planting* by Michael Littlewood

Pest controllers

COMMON NAME	BOTANICAL NAME	TYPE	CONTROLS
Elderberry	*Sambucus*	S	Aphids, carrot flies, cucumber beetles, peach tree borers, root maggots
Eucalyptus	*Eucalyptus*	T	General insecticide
Fennel	*Foeniculum vulgare*	H	Deters aphids
French marigold	*Tagetes patula*	F	Deters Mexican bean beetles, nematodes
Garlic	*Allium sativum*	V	Against a whole range of pests including aphids, caterpillars, codling moths, Japanese beetles
Horseradish	*Armoracia rusticana*	V	Fungicide for fruit trees, deters Colorado beetles
Horsetail	*Equisetum*	F	Slugs and snails
Hyssop	*Hyssopus officinalis*	H	Repels flea beetles, insect larvae
Ivy	*Hedera helix*	F	Corn wireworms
Lavender cotton	*Santolina chamaesyparissus*	F	Deters corn wireworms and southern rootworms
Leek	*Allium ampeloprasum*	V	Deters carrot flies
Marigold	*Tagetes*	H	Reduces nematodes, cabbage pests
Milkweed	*Asclepias*		Deters aphids
Mint	*Mentha*	H	Colorado beetles, ants
Mustard	*Brassica nigra*	V	Reduces aphids
Nasturtium	*Tropaaeolum majus*	F	Reduces aphids, cabbage worms, Colorado beetles, squash bugs and whiteflies
Onion	*Allium cepa*	V	Deters Colorado beetles, carrot flies
Parsley	*Petroselinum crispum*	H	Asparagus beetles
Pelargonium	*Pelargonium*	F	Cabbage moths, corn earworms, and Japanese beetles
Peppers	*Capsicum*	V	General insect repellent
Petunia	*Petunia*	F	Repels Mexican bean beetles, potato bugs, and squash bugs
Pot marigold	*Calendula officinalis*	F	Deters asparagus beetles, tomato hornworms
Potato	*Solanum tuberosum*	V	Deters Mexican bean beetles

Type: F = Flower H = Herb S = Shrub T = Tree V = Vegetable

Pest controllers

COMMON NAME	BOTANICAL NAME	TYPE	CONTROLS
Radish	*Raphanus sativus*	V	Deters cucumber beetles, root flies, vine borers, and many others
Ragweed	*Ambrosia artemisiifolia*		Reduces flea beetles
Rhubarb	*Rheum rhabarbarum*	V	General insecticide, blackspot
Rosemary	*Rosmarinus officinalis*	H	Deters bean beetles, cabbage moths, carrot flies, and many other insects
Rue	*Ruta graveolens*	H	Deters beetles and fleas
Rye	*Secale*	V	Reduces nematodes
Sage	*Salvia officinalis*	H	Cabbage worms, cabbage moths, and root maggots
Savory	*Satureja*	H	Deters Mexican bean beetles
Scorzonera	*Scorzonera hispanica*	V	Deters carrot flies
Southernwood	*Artemisia abrotanum*		Deters cabbage moths, carrot flies
Soybean	*Glycine max*	V	Deters corn earworms, corn borers
Spurry	*Spergula arvensis*		Reduces aphids, caterpillars, and root worms
Sudan grass	*Sorghum sudanense*		Reduces Williamette mites on vines
Tansy	*Tanecetum vulgare*	F	Deters many insects including ants, aphids, cabbage worms, Colorado beetles, Japanese beetles, squash bugs
Thyme	*Thymus vulgaris*	H	Cabbage worms, cabbage loopers, whiteflies
Tomato	*Lycopersicon lycopersicum*	F	Asparagus beetles, loopers, flea beetles, and whiteflies on cabbage
Wormwood	*Artemisia*		General insecticide; deters mice and other rodents, slugs and snails

Type: F = Flower H = Herb V = Vegetable

Source: *Companion Planting* by Michael Littlewood

HOST AND DECOY PLANTS

Hosts to Insects

Many of the predators that live off insect pests can be attracted to the garden by incorporating in it plants that they like. Their presence will never rid the garden of pests, but it will help to keep them at tolerable levels.

Decoy Plants

Some plants act as alternative food sources for pests, distracting them away from the main crop plant. Careful placement of these decoy plants is necessary, otherwise they may do just the opposite of what is intended and entice the pests onto the main crops.

Decoy Plants

COMMON NAME	BOTANICAL NAME	INSECTS THEY ATTRACT
Alfalfa, or lucerne	*Medicago sativa*	Lygus bugs
Amaranth (pigweed)	*Amaranthus*	Ground beetles
Anise	*Pimpinella anisum*	Beneficial wasps
Blackberry	*Rubus*	Anagrus epos
Black nightshade	*Solanum nigrum*	Colorado beetles
Celery (flowers)	*Apium graveolens*	Beneficial wasps
Chamomile	*Chamaemelum nobile*	Hoverflies, beneficial wasps and others
Chervil	*Anthriscus cerefolium*	Hoverflies, beneficial wasps and others
Clover	*Trifolium*	Ground beetles, parasites of woolly apple aphids
Dandelion	*Taraxacum officinale*	Beneficial wasps
Fat hen, or lamb's quarters	*Chenopodium album*	Leafminers
Fennel	*Foeniculum vulgare*	Hoverflies, beneficial wasps
Goldenrod	*Solidago*	Hoverflies, praying mantis, and other predators
Hawthorn	*Crataegus*	Diamondback moth parasites
Hyssop	*Hyssopus officinalis*	Cabbage butterflies
Ivy	*Hedera helix*	Hoverflies, beneficial wasps
Jimsonweed, or thorn apple	*Datura stramonium*	Colorado beetles
Marigold	*Tagetes*	Hoverflies
Milkweed	*Asclepias*	Several parasites
Mint	*Menthe*	Hoverflies and several wasps and other beneficial insects
Mustard	*Brassica hirta*	Cabbage butterflies and various parasites
Peanut	*Arachis hypogaea*	Predatory spiders on *Ostrinia furnacalis*
Ragweed	*Ambrosia*	Parasites for oriental fruit moths and strawberry leaf rollers
Soybean	*Glycine max*	Trichogramma wasps
Spurry	*Spergula arvensis*	Several insects that prey on cabbage pest
Stinging nettle	*Urtica dioica*	Many beneficial insects that prey on cabbage pests
Strawberry	*Fragaria*	Parasites of the oriental fruit moth
Sunflower	*Helianthus*	Lacewings, beneficial wasps
Tansy	*Tanacetum vulgare*	Ladybirds
Yarrow	*Achillea*	Ladybirds, predatory wasps

PLANT PESTS

VEGETABLE	SYMPTOMS	CAUSE
Bean	Stunted growth and obvious signs of blackfly notches eaten from margins of leaves	Black bean aphids Weevils
Beet	Blotches or blisters on the leaves	Leafminers
Cabbage	Small holes in leaves Large holes in leaves Silvery holes on underside of the leaves Yellowing, curling leaves with waxy, grey insects Weakening plants with sooty moulds, honeydew and obvious signs of whitefly Wilting leaves and tunnelled roots Wilting leaves and tunnelled stems	Flea beetles Caterpillars or slugs Diamond-back moths Mealy aphids Cabbage whiteflies Cabbage root flies Flea beetles
Carrot	Tunnelling in the roots, wilting leaves, turning yellow	Carrot root flies
Celery	Blotches or blisters on the leaves	Leafminers
Cucumber	Yellowing and nodules on the roots Holes in the cucumber	Nematodes Slugs or snails
Lettuce	Holes in leaves Stunted growth, yellowing leaves, white powdery patches on roots Stunted growth, yellowing leaves, lumps on the roots Sticky honeydew and obvious signs of aphids	Slugs or snails Root aphids Nematodes Greenflies
Onion	Leaves drooping, turning yellow Swollen and distorted leaves	Onion flies Nematodes
Parsnip	Tunnelling in the roots, wilting leaves turning yellow	Carrot flies
Pea	Silvery patches on leaves and pods Notches eaten from margins of leaves Stunted growth and obvious signs of greenfly on stems	Thrips Weevils Greenflies

Plant pests continued

VEGETABLE	SYMPTOMS	CAUSE
Potato	Browning leaves and obvious signs of aphids Brown spots and holes in leaves Weak and stunted plants with dying lower leaves Small holes and tunnels in tubers Large holes in tubers Leaves eaten, black excreta and obvious signs of black and yellow beetles and their red larvae	Greenflies Capsid bugs Nematodes Wireworms Slugs Colorado beetle
Summer squash	Yellowing and nodules on the roots Holes in the summer squash	Nematodes Slugs, snails or mice
Tomato	Stunted growth and wilted leaves, lumps on the roots Stunted and curled leaves, sticky honeydew Holes in fruit	Nematodes Whiteflies slugs

TRAPS, BARRIERS AND DETERRENTS

Many garden pests can be trapped or kept at bay using relatively inexpensive materials and sometimes recycled household items. Put the barriers in place when the plants are young and always ensure that pests are not trapped inside the barrier.

CONTROL METHOD	HOW IT WORKS
Beer traps and deterrents (granules, copper strips and greasebands)	Traps are an effective way of both controlling pests, such as slugs, and finding out which ones are actually present. A deterrent is a physical barrier over which the pest cannot or will not pass. There are many types and their effectiveness can vary.
Bug nets in the greenhouse	Greenhouse vents are problematic in terms of pest control in that they allow both pests in and purchased biological controls out. Bug nets can stop this happening.
Fleece stretched over a crop or as a small wall 60cm (24in) high	Can be used to create a favourable microclimate around young plants. Also acts as a barrier to airborne pests, such as carrot fly. On the downside, it can also keep out airborne predators from pests that overwinter in the soil.
Fruit nets over fruit	Especially useful for summer soft fruit crops, which can quickly be devastated by birds.
Individual cloches	Can act as a barrier to a wide variety of airborne pests. Any pests that are sealed into this environment may, however, find the perfect environment in which to thrive.
Mesh cages for trees	Used to keep rabbits and hares at bay. The cage is usually a simple construction formed from three or more stakes driven into the ground, with chicken wire (or similar) attached to them.
Rabbit fencing	A continuous barrier to prevent rabbits entering areas where plants are growing. The base of the wire should be buried below ground level to prevent the rabbits burrowing a passage beneath it.
Bird scarers (for example, scarecrows)	Bird scarers have the drawback of a limited lifespan before the birds learn that they are not a real threat. They can, of course, be changed and most bird scarers are only needed on a seasonal basis.

Traps, barriers and deterrents continued

CONTROL METHOD	HOW IT WORKS
String or wire netting stretched over seedlings (for example, peas)	Aerial barriers can protect against bird attack. They may only be needed for the duration of the crop's life, or even less.
Traps (sticky, coloured strips used in the greenhouse)	Can provide a certain degree of control against the flying adults of insect pests. Less effective than they are sometimes thought to be, they are of more use for showing whether a particular pest is present or not, thereby allowing other control measures to be put in place.
Traps (pheromone)	Used to detect the presence of insects. The pheromones attract members of the opposite sex and the appearance of the target species allows gardeners to begin looking for and controlling the young that cause the damage.
Tree guards (spiral)	Spiral guards are useful for protecting the bark of newly planted trees from rabbits and hares, especially in winter and early spring. These guards expand as the tree develops, but they are best removed completely after about a year.
Tree shelter	Protects newly planted trees from vertebrate pests and from the worst rigours of the environment by providing a favourable microclimate around them. They naturally degrade under the action of sunlight, but are best removed after two to three years.
Twiggy branches over plants	Arched over young plants, these can be an effective deterrent to pests such as birds and cats. They do not prevent the migration of beneficial predators to the plants.

ORGANIC CONTROLS

PRODUCT	PEST/DISEASE	ADVANTAGES	DISADVANTAGES
Bacillus thuringiensis	Caterpillars	• Bacterial spores that produce a toxic protein that is useful against caterpillars but will not cause any harm to beneficials. • Works quickly, paralysing the caterpillar and so preventing any further damage.	• Quickly degrades in sunlight and needs frequent re-application throughout the growing season.
Bordeaux mixture	Blights, leaf spots (on beet, brassicas, celery, spinach)	• An inorganic chemical allowed under organic standards as it is not harmful to humans or soil life. • Effective against potato blight, peach leaf curl, raspberry cane spot and many other fungal diseases	• A preventive, not a cure, and must be applied thoroughly and in good time.
Derris/Rotenone	Aphids (greenfly, blackfly), beetles (flea beetle, pollen beetle), small caterpillars, turnip fly, weevils, red spider mite, sucking insects – see aphids, thrips	• Liquid or dust, which kills most insects, but is particularly effective against mites. • Treat wasps' nests by puffing the dust into the entrance at dusk; repeat after a week.	• Indiscriminate in action. • Lethal to fish, pigs and tortoises. • Breaks down in sunlight. • Slower to act than pyrethrum. • Currently under review and no longer recommended for use in UK and elsewhere.
Insecticidal soap	Aphids, leafhoppers, red spider mite, whitefly	• The preferred pesticide and even more effective than soft soap. • Safe to use and made from natural products.	• Ineffective against larger insect pests.
Pyrethrum/ Pyrethrins	Caterpillars, beetles (many), greenfly, blackfly, leafhoppers, whitefly, thrips	• Useful for killing many insect pests.	• No longer available in pure form and commonly supplied with a synthetic synergist. • Kills beneficial insects and fish (but is safe for mammals).
Quassia	Aphids, small caterpillars, sawfly grubs, mites	• Solution (made from a tree bark) that kills aphids but is harmless to bees and other beneficial insects. • Sold combined with Derris, which makes both more effective.	• No longer available on its own.
Soft soap	Aphids	• Traditionally used as a spray to kill aphids, red spider mites, mealy bugs, whiteflies and other pests.	
Sulphur	Powdery mildew	• The pure element is allowed under organic standards as a control for powdery mildews on fruit, flowers and vegetables and for preventing rots in overwintering bulbs and tubers.	• Take care when using it with fruit trees and bushes as a few varieties are allergic to sulphur.

Sprays — Safety Rules

DO

- Store the sprays away from children, in the original labelled containers.
- Wash equipment thoroughly afterwards, having disposed of any leftovers.
- Keep all sprays locked away in a cupboard.
- Spray in still weather to avoid drift.
- Use protective gloves, mask and goggles.
- Spray only when necessary.
- Follow the manufacturer's instructions precisely.
- Spray only on windless evenings when the good insects will have retired for the night.

DO NOT

- Eat sprayed plants for two weeks.
- Spray open flowers for fear of harming bees.
- Store any leftover spray.
- Use the same equipment for feeding.

Legal Considerations

It is illegal to use any pesticide that has not been officially approved by law. In the United Kingdom, organic gardeners may use the following:

Insecticides

- Bacillius thuringiensis (Bt)
- Insecticidal soap
- Pyrethrum
- Rape oil
- Derris

Fungicides

- Bordeaux mixture (copper based)
- Sulphur

Quassia, neem and garlic oil are not registered for use in the UK

Biological Pest Controls

PEST	AGENT	SPECIAL REQUIREMENTS
Glasshouse whitefly	*Encarsia formosa* (parasitic wasp)	Optimum temperature 18–25°C (64–77°F)
Red spider mite	*Phytoselulus persimilis* (predatory mite)	Optimum temperature 18–25°C (64–77°F) Humidity 60%
Mealybug	*Cryptolaemus montrouzieri* (predatory beetle)	Optimum temperature 20–25°C (66–77°F) Humidity 70%
Aphids	*Aphidoletes aphidimyza* (predatory midge larva)	Optimum temperature 21°C (70°F) Humidity high 80%
Vine weevil	*Heterorhabditis megidis* (parasitic nematode)	Minimum soil temperature 14°C (57°F) Moist soil essential
Soft scale	*Metaphycus helvolus* (parasitic wasp)	Optimum temperature 20–30°C (68–86°F) Good light levels needed
Slugs	*Phasmarhabditis hermaphrodita* (parasitic nematode)	Minimum soil temperature 5°C (40°F) Moist soil essential
Thrips	*Amblyseus cucumeris* (predatory mite)	Optimum temperature 25°C (77°F)
Leatherjackets	*Steinernema feltiae* (parasitic nematode)	Minimum soil temperature 10°C (50°F) Moist soil essential
Chafer grubs	*Heterorhabditis megidis* (parasitic nematode)	Minimum soil temperature 12°C (54°F) Moist soil essential Apply from mid to late summer

Organic Sprays

Home Made

All sprays are dangerous. Those made from plants are generally less so than manufactured chemicals. Nevertheless, DO NOT make up solutions of nicotine (tobacco or chrysanthemum – though manufacturers uses these as a base for commercial insecticides – or any other plants the properties of which are uncertain. All sprays should be used with extreme caution and only when all other methods of control have failed. When preparing home made sprays do not use the kitchen blender or other kitchen utensils unless specifically reserved for this purpose. DO NOT EAT SPRAYED PLANTS FOR AT LEAST TWO WEEKS.

PLANT NAME	CONTROL FOR
Basil *Ocimum basilicum*	Aphids, asparagus beetles
Catnip *Nepeta cataria*	Colorado beetles
Chestnut *Castanea sativa*	Beet moths
Chive *Allium schoenoprasum*	Apple scab, mildew on cucumbers, gooseberries, summer squash and pumpkins
Citrus fruit *Citrus*	Fall armyworms and bollworms
Coriander *Coriandrum sativum*	Aphids, spider mites
Elderberry *Sambucus*	Aphids, carrot flies, cucumber beetles, peach tree borers, root maggots
Eucalyptus *Eucalyptus*	General insecticide
Garlic *Allium sativum*	Against a whole range of pests including aphids, caterpillars, codling moths, Japanese beetles, root maggots, rusts, snails
Horseradish *Armozacia rusticana*	Fungicide for fruit trees
Horsetail *Equisetum*	Slugs and snails
Ivy *Hedera helix*	Corn wireworms
Mint *Mentha*	Colorado beetles, ants
Parsley *Petroselinum crispum*	Asparagus beetles
Pelargonium *Pelargonium*	Cabbage moths, corn earworms and Japanese beetles
Pepper *Capsicum*	General insect repellent
Rhubarb *Rheum rhabarbarum*	General insecticide, blackspot
Johnson grass *Sorghum halepense*	Willamette mites on vines
Sage *Salvia officinalis*	Cabbage worms
Southernwood *Artemisia abrotanum*	Cabbage worms
Thyme *Thymus vulgaris*	Cabbage worms
Tomato *Lycopersicon lycopersicum*	Asparagus beetles
Wormwood *Artemisia*	Fleas

MULCHING

Mulching is essential for the protection of soil in the organic garden. It offers a number of benefits and a variety of materials, both natural and man-made, can be used. Mulching, like composting, is a basic practice of organic gardeners.

Benefits

- Suppresses weeds and prevents weed seed germination.
- Conserves soil moisture.
- Maintains a stable soil temperature – cooler in summer and warmer in winter.
- Improves soil fertility and texture.
- Protects soils from heavy rainfalls.
- Keeps soil from being splashed on to plants by rain or irrigation.
- Protects less hardy plants from frosts.
- Encourages earthworm activity.
- Root crops easier to lift in winter if mulched.
- Keeps soil off trailing crops.

Application

- Mulches can be applied at any time, except when the soil is very wet or dry or cold.
- The best time to mulch is when planting or when the soil is warm and moist.
- The thicker the mulch the better, from 50–100mm (2–4in) deep depending upon the material being used and the type of crop and its growth at the time.
- Mulches can be left, or removed from the garden.
- Remove all weeds before mulching.
- Leave a circle around the base of a plant so that soil remains dry and open to the air and rotting of plant 'neck' is avoided, except for brassicas and tomatoes.
- Do not mulch in wet, low-lying areas.

Materials

All organic materials should be well rotted or nitrogen will be taken from the soil, especially in the early stages of decomposition and at springtime.

1. These cannot be used unless they have had time to break down over many months.

- Wood
- Tree bark – pulverized or shredded
- Sawdust
- Pine needles
- Wood shavings
- Prunings
- Wood chips

Mulch materials come in two forms: loose, like those in the first and second list, and membranes (in the third list).

2. These can contribute to the improvement of the soil and can be used as they become available.

- Well-rotted animal manure
- Stack bottom hay and straw
- Mushroom compost
- Seaweed
- Grass clippings (dry)
- Hop wastes
- Leaves
- Sheep fleeces
- Wool shoddy
- Coco shells (imported product)

3. Other materials can be used for mulching but they will not add to the fertility of the soil.

- Layers of newspapers and cardboard
- Old insulation material made from natural products
- Shredded newspapers
- Do not use paper printed with coloured inks.
- Old carpets made from natural fibres
- Man-made – plastic film, black and white perforated and unperforated

The above should be covered with a layer of the materials given in the first and second lists. Lay plastic after a good rainfall or watering.

Black plastic film materials are more often used to suppress weeds and conserve moisture.

White/clear plastic film is often used to warm up soils or to reflect light on to a plant, thereby encouraging growth and ripening. Film encourages slugs, mice and voles.

Note:

LEAVES:

Leaves provide an excellent mulch. Shredded leaves do not mat down, and enrich the soil more quickly than whole leaves. There is rarely any nitrogen deficiency in leaves, so it is not necessary to apply nitrogen to the soil before mulching. If unshredded, leaves should be mixed with straw or some other light material so that they do not become a soggy mass.

SAWDUST:

Sawdust makes a very good mulch. For blueberries, use a sawdust from softwoods as a mulch. There will be less packing down and better aeration, and the blueberries prefer an acidic soil. Try banking hardwood sawdust around the base of old apple trees as a means of rejuvenating them. To counteract the nitrogen deficiency inherent in sawdust, add compost to the soil before mulching.

Beware of loose materials, such as cocoa shells and bark, which can be easily blown away and/or may be scattered by birds. Many materials can be aesthetically pleasing and can enhance the productive garden. Some materials, such as bark or wood chips, can be used for paths.

Mulch chart

MATERIAL	USE	APPLICATION	MAIN USE
Leafmould	On seed beds Around bedding plants, herbs, herbaceous plants	In autumn before sowing Any time when soil conditions are suitable	Improves soil structure Improves soil structure and moisture and looks attractive
Compost	On vegetable crops with a long growing period Around herbaceous plants	When well established and still actively growing In spring	Provides nutrients and retains moisture Provides nutrients, retains moisture and improves soil structure
Worm compost	On plants in pots or individual garden plants that need feeding	When making quick growth, usually in spring	Provides nutrients, particularly oxygen
Well-rotted manure	Around plants that need a lot of feeding	When making quick growth, usually in spring	Provides nutrients, particularly nitrogen
Grass clippings	Around widely spaced vegetable crops	Any time when soil conditions are suitable	Controls weeds and keeps in moisture
Shredded prunings	Around trees and shrubs On paths	Any time when soil conditions are suitable Any time	Protects soil surface and controls weeds Keeps the surface clean
Bark/wood chips	Around trees and shrubs Around fruit on the ground	Any time when soil conditions are suitable Before fruit forms	Protects soil surface and controls weeds; visually pleasing
Straw*	Between widely spaced shrubs, fruit trees and bushes On paths	Any time when soil conditions are suitable Any time	Keeps fruit clean and retains moisture Controls weeds and retains moisture Keeps surfaces clean and tidy
Hay*	Around fruit trees, canes and bushes	In late spring	Controls weeds, provides nutrients and retains moisture
Cocoa shell	Around bedding and herbaceous plants	When in active growth	Controls weeds, looks attractive and retains moisture
Sawdust/wood shavings	On paths	Any time	Keeps surfaces clean and tidy

**preferably semi-rotted*

WEED MANAGEMENT

SPECIES	ABP	WEED RATING	USES	SPECIFIC USE	HOW TO CONTROL
Bindweed	P	*****			Heavy mulch; then dig
Bracken	P	***	DA	K/P/Mn/Cu/Co	Raise pH
Brambles	P	***	E	Berries	Cut repeatedly
Creeping buttercup	P	****			Improve drainage
Celandine	P	*****			Very hard if established. Dig/mulch/dig
Chickweed	A	*	E/GC/DA	E: young leaves GC: green manure DA: K/P/Mn	Mulch
Coltsfoot	P	***	DA	S/Mg/Ca/K/Fe/Cu	Raise pH. Cut repeatedly
Couchgrass	P	*****			Fork, cut, mulch
Dandelion	P	***	E/I/DA	Salad; as spinach DA: Na/Si/Mg/Ca/K/P/Fe/Cu	Pull or dig
Deadnettle	P	**	I		Mulch, pull, fork
Docks	P	***	DA	Ca/K/P/Fe	Dig deep
Goosegrass	A	**	CP		Pull before seeds
Ground elder	P	*****			Heavy mulch, then dig (repeatedly)
Hedge garlic	A	*	E/I	E: young leaves	Pull late if at all
Horsetail	P	*****	AFA/DA	Powdered leaf tea spray for mildew; DA:Si/Mg/Ca/Fe	Very hard if established. Improve drainage/sharp sand/rake out
Mosses	P	***			Improve drainage/sharp sand/rake out
Salad burnet	A	*	E/DA	Young leaf in salad DA:Fe	
Shepherd's purse	A	*	CP/DA	Na/S/Ca	Pull before seeds/mulch
Sow thistle	A	*	CP/DA	Mn/K/Cu	Pull before seeds
Speedwell	A	**			Mulch
Caper spurge	A	*	DA	B: said to repel moles	Mulch or hoe
Stinging nettle	P	***	E/CP/DA/GC	E: young leaves as spinach. DA: Na/S/N/Ca/K/Fe/Cu	Cut, dig, mulch/dig
Rosebay willowherb	P	***	CP/DA		Fork/cut/fork
Yarrow	P	*		CP: increases pest resistance in neighbours. DA:S/Ca/K/Cu	Fork/cut/pull

Weed rating refers to difficulty of control. A = Annual, B = Bi-annual, P = Perennial. Uses: AFA = anti-fungal agent; CP = companion plant; DA = dynamic accumulator; E = Edible; GC = garden compost; I = attracts insects.
Timing is important; disposal of non-invasive plants can be done before seed set.
Source: *The Natural Garden Book*

Materials for weed control

Loose materials

Cocoa shells
Waste product of the chocolate industry. Apply in a layer at least 5cm (2in) deep. Water lightly after application to moisten surface. Higher in nitrogen than wood-based mulches.

Gravel and slate waste
Good around plants that like dry, hot conditions.

Leafmould
A home-made, short-term mulch. Best used over a membrane.

Municipal compost – coarse grade
Recycle green waste. Quicker to degrade than bark or wood chips.

Sawdust
Use rotted only to avoid nitrogen deficiency.

Shredded paper
Wet before using, preferably mix with other materials.

Straw and hay
Informal appearance. Should last for a season. Use a layer 15cm (6in) thick. Hay will feed plants as it decays, but may produce its own crop of seedling weeds.

Tree bark
Attractive dark-coloured mulch.

Wood chips
Forest waste, or chipped scrap wood. Available in stained colours. Lower cost than bark. Apply a high-nitrogen fertilizer before mulching young plants.

Woody plant prunings (shredded)
Home produced or from a tree contractor. Compost for a few months before use, or use fresh on paths.

Solid materials

Black polythene sheeting (400-800 gauge)
Suitable only as a ground-clearing mulch. Do not cover ground for more than a few months without removing the polythene to allow air and water into the soil. Hold in place by burying edges in the ground or weighting with heavy items.

Cardboard
No-cost option for a single season. Lay on soil, overlapping well to prevent weeds growing through. Keep in place with straw or hay. Vigorous plants such as pumpkins can be planted through the cardboard.

Carpet (used)
Use only wool carpet.

Coir matting
3-5 year lifespan, no need to cover it. Hold in place with wire staples or fixing pegs.

Newspaper
No-cost option for a single season. Lay opened out newspapers, at lease 8 sheets thick, around and between existing plants. Top with grass cuttings or leafmould to keep in place.

Paper mulch
Sturdy paper in a roll, for use on annual vegetable beds.

Synthetic spun fabric
Long-term weed control. Cover with loose mulch to protect from light.

Woven plastic
Medium-term weed control. Cover with loose mulch to extend life.

7 THE TASKS

- Storage
- Monthly Reminder

STORAGE

VEGETABLE	METHOD	TIME	VARIETY, CULTIVATION, SPECIAL TREATMENT
Artichoke, Jerusalem	In situ		Plant tubers, dig to eat after tops brown, leave some for next year's crop.
Asparagus	Freeze	6 months	Well-drained perennial site, harvest very young, blanch briefly.
Beans (green)	Freeze or Salt	6-12 months	Snap or scarlet runner. Pick young, (green) salt, blanch briefly or salt.
Beans	Dry	6-12 months	Leave pods on vine long as possible, then hang to complete drying. Store airtight.
Beets	Clamp	3-4 months	Twist of leaves (don't cut), put large beets at bottom to store longer.
Broccoli	Freeze	3 months	Blanch thick stems well, steaming tops.
Brussels sprouts	In situ or Freeze	2-3 months 6-12 months	Winter crop, freeze surplus when sprouts are small and tight.
Cabbage, red	Pickle or Freeze	4-5 months 12 months	Winter crop, pickle for variety. Freeze cooked for convenience, long store.
Cabbage, green	Sauerkraut	12 months	White Dutch or similar, ferment in traditional manner.
Cabbage, savoy	In situ	2-3 months	Stand until cropped
Cabbage, winter/red	Hang cool, dry	2-3 months	Hang firm early-winter cabbages in dry nets, after removing outer leaves.
Carrots	Clamp		Maincrop/late varieties.

VEGETABLE	METHOD	TIME	VARIETY, CULTIVATION, SPECIAL TREATMENT
Garlic	Hang dry	4-6 months	Plant cloves earlier than onion sets in dry, sunny spot.
Herbs	Dried	4-6 months	Pick early but dry, hang in shade or oven-dry, crumble into boxes when dry.
Leeks	In situ	3-4 months	Long-term planting in deeply cultivated soil. Pull when required, to late winter.
Maize	Freeze	6-12 months	Plant solid square for good pollination. Blanch (and cool) well for storage.
Mushrooms	Extract Dry		Salt-extracted "essence" for sauces. Slow-dry in oven or sun. Store sealed.
Onions	Hang dry	4-6 months	Ripen well, with roots loosened, before lifting. Beware neck rot.
Parsnips	Freeze young Clamp rest	6-12 months	Deep, well-cultivated soil not young recently fertilized. Lift young for freezing. Older roots best frosted before use.
Peas	Freeze	12+ months	Any variety, blanch briefly after shelling. Sugarsnap, unblanched but shorter storage.
Potatoes	Store dark	3-4 months	Maincrop or late. Best stored in paper sacks. Discard any green tubers.
Rutabagas	Store dark	3 months	Maincrop.
Sunflower	Dry seed	6-9 months	Collect ripe seed, store dry or roasted.
Turnips	Store dark Freeze	3-4 months 9-12 months	Maincrop. Young tender roots, part-cooked.
Winter squash	Hang, dry	2-4 months	Late variety. Becomes dry during long/squash dry storage.

January

MID-WINTER

MONTHLY REMINDER

VEGETABLES

SOWING

GREENHOUSE/FRAME/CLOCHE

Early peas and broad beans.

GREENHOUSE HEATED

Cauliflower - early varieties
Onions
Leeks
Strawberries - Alpine
Planting
Rhubarb

HARVESTING

GROUND

Kale, leeks, cabbage, savoys, parsnip, cauliflower, Brussels sprouts, celery, Chinese and Jerusalem artichokes, celeriac, chicories, endive, parsley, radish, salsify, scorzonera, spinach, Swiss chard.

STORE

Roots, apples, Jerusalem artichokes, beetroot, carrots, garlic, onions, potatoes (maincrop), marrows, shallots, swedes, turnips, winter radish, salsify, scorzonera.

Check for deterioration.

FORCED

Seakale, chicory.

FORCING

Rhubarb, salsify, seakale.

GROUND WORKING

Spread compost on vacant land. Prepare ground if not too wet.

Hoe between growing crops when dry, unless already mulched.

GENERAL

Order seeds and seed potatoes. Make cropping plan of the plot.

Burn woody rubbish in a slow smother fire.

FRUIT

PLANTING

Plant trees, bushes and canes when conditions allow.

Check all tree stakes and ties.

PRUNING

Established trees (except in severe frost)

Collect and shred prunings.

Newly planted cane fruits.

FERTILIZING

Apply potash to strawberries, gooseberries and red and white currants. Apply balanced fertilizer to cobnuts and filberts.

PROTECTING

Cover wall trained peach trees to prevent peach leaf curl.

SPRAYING

All trees, canes and bushes with winterwash, protecting nearby grass and crops.

All fruit trees and bushes with diluted elder solution.

INSPECTING

Check all apple and pear trees for canker and treat if necessary.

HARVESTING

Check fruit in store for any deterioration and infection.

GENERAL

Inspect stakes and ties of newly planted trees especially after gales.

MONTHLY REMINDER

February LATE-WINTER

VEGETABLES

SOWING

GREENHOUSE/FRAME/CLOCHE
Brussels sprouts, broad beans, peas, carrots, turnips, radishes.

GREENHOUSE - HEATED
Tomatoes, cauliflower, celery, French beans, aubergine.

PLANTING

OUTDOOR
Jerusalem artichoke, rhubarb, garlic, shallots, seakale onions (sets).

FERTILIZING

Dress asparagus bed with a general organic fertilizer.

Feed spring cabbages.

HARVESTING

GROUND
Chinese and Jerusalem artichokes, sprouting broccoli, brassicas, Brussels sprouts, cabbage (winter), calabrese, cauliflower (winter heading), celery, kale, oriental greens, celeriac, chicories, endive, leeks, parsley, parsnip, radish, rhubarb, salsify, scorzonera, seakale, winter spinach, Swiss chard, salad plants.

GREENHOUSE - HEATED
Lettuce, mustard & cress, bean shoots, mushrooms.

STORE
Jerusalem artichoke, beetroot, carrots, garlic, bulb onions, potatoes (maincrop), shallots, swedes, turnips, winter radish, salsify, scorzonera.

FORCING

Rhubarb, salsify, seakale.

GROUND WORKING

Complete all digging, liming and manuring. Prepare for sowing. Incorporate compost.

GENERAL

Place seed potatoes in trays to sprout ('chit') in the light.

Cut bean and pea sticks.

FRUIT

PLANTING

Continue all planting of trees and bushes.

PRUNING

Raspberries - Cut down canes (autumn fruiting) to ground level. Cut down newly planted canes to 22-30cm (9-12in). Newly planted and established stone fruits (except pyramid plums - see April).

Apples and pears - Complete formative pruning of newly planted trees. Continue pruning established trees, except in hard frost.

Cobnuts and filberts - Prune provided catkins are fully open and releasing pollen - otherwise leave until March.

FERTILIZING

On light land apply potash if necessary to all trees and bushes, $33g/m^2$ ($1oz/yd^2$).

Apply nitrogen in early February to trees in grass.

Apply nitrogen in late February to trees in cultivated ground.

Apply compost or rotted manure around all trees and bushes as a mulch.

PROTECTING

Cover strawberries with cloches or tunnels early in the month.

Cover wall trained trees with draped hessian or equivalent against frost.

SPRAYING

Peaches and nectarines against peach leaf curl. Apply sticky bands to apple trees.

HARVESTING

Check and remove any rotten fruit in store.

INSPECTING

Check apples and pears for canker and treat if necessary.

General

Inspect stakes and ties of newly planted trees especially after gales.

MONTHLY REMINDER

March EARLY SPRING

VEGETABLES

SOWING

GREENHOUSE/FRAME/CLOCHE

Beetroot (globe), radishes, cabbage (summer), carrots, turnips, lettuce, French beans, cauliflower, salads.

GREENHOUSE - HEATED

Aubergine, celery (self blanching), celery, celeriac, cucumbers, peppers, tomatoes.

OUTDOOR

Broad beans, beetroot, Brussels sprouts, cabbage (summer and autumn), calabrese, texsel greens, carrots, chicory (sugar-loaf), leeks, kohlrabi, lettuce (summer), onions (bulb and spring), peas (early), radish (summer), salsify, scorzonera, spinach (summer), Swiss chard, turnips, salad plants.

PLANTING

Globe, Jerusalem and Chinese artichoke, onions (sets), onions (autumn sown), shallots, garlic, seakale, horse-radish, asparagus, potatoes (early), leeks.

FERTILIZING

Apply general fertilizer to all open ground. Apply nitrogen (30g to 1m row) to spring cabbage.

TRANSPLANTING

Cauliflower (early summer)

HARVESTING

GROUND

Cabbage (savoy), spring greens, sprouting broccoli, spinach, beet, Chinese & Jerusalem artichokes, Brussels sprouts, cabbage - winter, calabrese, cauliflower (winter and spring heading), kale, Oriental and Texsel greens, celeriac, chicories, endive, leeks, lettuce (winter protected), spring onion, parsley, parsnip, radish, rhubarb, salsify, scorzonera, seakale, spinach (winter), Swiss chard.

STORE

Beetroot, carrots, garlic, onions (bulb), potatoes (maincrop), shallots, swede, turnips, radish (winter), salsify, scorzonera.

FORCING

Chicory (whitloof), seakale

GROUND WORKING

Complete all digging, manuring and hoe to remove weed seedling. Check for slugs.

Place cloches in position one week before sowing.

Sow green manure on any vacant ground.

GENERAL

Check seed potatoes. Pinch top of broad beans when in flower to reduce attack from blackfly.

FRUIT

PLANTING

Complete planting trees and bushes. Perpetual varieties of strawberries (fruiting July onwards) and remove all blossoms until June (end).

PRUNING

Cobnuts and filberts - complete pruning.

Acid cherries - Cut out older wood on established trees

FERTILIZING

Apply potash to cane fruits. Complete mulching of young trees, bushes and canes. Apply nitrogen to blackcurrants. Give second application of nitrogen to pears in grass.

PROTECTING

Protect blossom and young fruitlets on still cold nights from frost damage.

SPRAYING

Peaches and nectarines against peach leaf curl. Apply sticky bands to apple trees.

INSPECTING

Inspect stakes and ties of newly planted trees - check for wind damage.

GENERAL

Remove any weeds around all bushes and trees.

MONTHLY REMINDER

April MID-SPRING

VEGETABLES

SOWING

GREENHOUSE/FRAME/CLOCHE

Aubergine, celery, endive, peppers, sweetcorn, French and runner beans, cucumbers (outdoor), marrow, courgettes, squashes, pumpkin, New Zealand spinach, tomatoes (outdoor).

GREENHOUSE - HEATED

French beans, cauliflower (early autumn).

OUTDOORS - UNPROTECTED

Asparagus pea, broad bean, sprouting broccoli, Brussels sprouts, cabbage (summer, autumn and winter), calabrese, Oriental greens (seedling crops and bolt resistant types), kale, carrots, chicory (red), kohlrabi, leeks, lettuce, onions (bulb and spring), parsnip, peas (maincrop), radish (summer), salsify, scorzonera, spinach, Swiss chard, turnip, salad plants.

PLANTING

Chinese, globe and Jerusalem Artichokes, asparagus, onions (bulb pot raised), onions (sets), potatoes (early and maincrop).

TRANSPLANTING

Cabbage (red), cauliflower, leek, broad beans.

FERTILIZING

Feed cabbages with high nitrogen fertilizer.

HARVESTING

GROUND

Jerusalem artichoke, asparagus, sprouting broccoli, spring cabbage, cauliflower (spring heading), texel greens, celeriac, chicory, endive, leek, spring onion, parsley, radish (summer and winter), rhubarb, salsify, scorzonera, seakale, spinach (winter), Swiss chard, salad plants, Oriental greens, (seedling crops).

STORE

Garlic, onions (bulb), potatoes (maincrop) , shallots.

FORCING

Chicory (witloof), seakale.

PROTECTING

Lettuce, early potatoes using fleece, tomatoes (outdoor).

GROUND WORKING

Hoe to remove all weeds from crops. Uproot and dispose of old brassica stumps. Earth up early potatoes. Prepare trenches for celery. Prepare sites for marrow, pumpkin, squash.

FRUIT

PLANTING

Complete strawberries by middle of month.

PRUNING

Plums (pyramid) - prune in early years.

Gooseberries, currants - (red and white) prune where necessary.

Figs - prune as necessary (warm areas of country).

FERTILIZING

Apply nitrogen (light dressing) to strawberries if growth is poor. Commence foliar feeding with seaweed extract at least every two weeks.

PROTECTING

Early flowering fruits with appropriate materials if frost is forecast. Uncover immediately so that pollination is ensured. Spray against pests and diseases using natural products wherever possible. Check netting for bird protection.

SPRAYING

Peaches and nectarines against peach leaf curl. Apply sticky bands to apple trees.

WATERING

Water all newly planted trees, bushes and canes if necessary.

GENERAL

Untie and retrain branches of wall trained fig trees where protection has been given. Hand pollinate wall trained peach and nectarine flowers. Mist spray at mid-day to help setting in dry climatic periods. Control weeds around all trees, bushes, canes.

MONTHLY REMINDER

May LATE SPRING

VEGETABLES

SOWING

GREENHOUSE/FRAME/CLOCHE

French beans, tomatoes, cucumbers (ridge), marrows.

Greenhouse – Heated

OUTDOORS

Asparagus pea, broad beans, French beans and runner beans, cabbage (summer), calabrese (autumn and winter), cauliflower (autumn), heading (winter and spring), Chinese and sprouting broccoli, kale, texsel greens, carrots, chicory (witloof), endive, Florence fennel, kohlrabi, leeks, lettuce, marrow, courgettes, squashes, pumpkins, spring onions, parsnips, pea (maincrop), radish, salsify, scorzonera, seakale, spinach (ordinary and New Zealand), swedes, turnips, salad plants.

PLANTING

UNPROTECTED

Jerusalem artichoke, aubergine, celeriac, celery, endive, lettuce, parsley, peppers, potatoes (early and maincrop), seakale, tomatoes (outdoor).

PROTECTED

Cucumber (outdoor), peppers, aubergine, sweetcorn, tomatoes (outdoor).

TRANSPLANTING

Brussels Sprouts, cabbage (summer and autumn), cauliflower (summer).

HARVESTING

GROUND

Asparagus, broad beans, sprouting broccoli, cabbage (spring), cauliflower (spring heading), texsel greens, carrots, celeriac, chicory (sugar loaf), endive kohlrabi, lettuce, spring onions, peas (early), radish, rhubarb, salsify, scorzonera, spinach (summer and winter), Swiss chard, turnips, salad plants.

STORE

Garlic, potatoes (maincrop), shallots.

PROTECTING

Pinch out tops of broad beans if attacked by blackfly.

SPRAYING

Be ready to spray against pests with natural products.

WATERING

Cauliflowers with diluted liquid manure and celery.

GROUND WORKING

Thin crops where applicable. Weed and mulch wherever necessary. Have materials ready for frost protection. Stake peas, earth-up potatoes.

FRUIT

PLANTING

Set out companion plants (annuals) around all trees and bushes.

PRUNING

Thin gooseberries.

FERTILIZING

Apply nitrogen (light dressing) to strawberries if growth is poor. Commence foliar feeding with seaweed extract at least every two weeks.

PROTECTING

Protect blossoms from frost. Protect soft fruits from birds with netting.

Mulch strawberry plants with straw to keep fruit off the ground.

Shorten leaders of all mature trees grown in a restricted form.

Put out codling moths.

WATERING

Ensure adequate water to all plants after flowering, especially those trained against walls.

HARVESTING

Green gooseberries, strawberries (under cloches).

GENERAL

De-blossom newly planted trees. De-shoot peaches and nectarines (wall trained).

Remove shoots on plums and damsons (wall trained) growing towards or away from wall.

De-blossom spring planted runners of summer fruiting strawberries.
Remove any weeds growing around any bushes, trees or vines.
Check all plants for pests, diseases and dieback.

Remove tied-on grease bands.

MONTHLY REMINDER

June EARLY SUMMER

VEGETABLES

SOWING

GREENHOUSE/FRAME/CLOCHE
Sweetcorn, aubergine, tomatoes.

OUTDOORS
French beans and runner beans, beetroot, calabrese, Chinese broccoli, cabbage (Chinese), Oriental greens and texsel greens, chicories, endive, Florence fennel, kohlrabi, lettuce, marrow, courgette, squash, pumpkin, spring onion, parsley, peas (maincrop), radish (summer), swedes, turnips, salad plants.

PLANTING

UNPROTECTED
Celery, tomatoes.

PROTECTED
Sweetcorn.

TRANSPLANTING

Sprouting broccoli, Brussels sprouts, cabbage (summer, autumn and winter), cauliflower (early autumn and autumn), leeks.

HARVESTING

GROUND
Asparagus pea, broad beans, French beans, beetroot, cabbage - (spring and summer), calabrese, cauliflower (spring heading and early summer), texsel greens, carrots, chicory (sugar-loaf), endive, kohlrabi, lettuce, onions (bulb - autumn sown), spring onions, parsley, peas (early and maincrop), potatoes (early), radish, rhubarb, spinach (summer), Swiss chard, turnip, salad plants.

STORE
Garlic, shallots.

PROTECTING

Check for pests and diseases.

WATERING

Ensure adequate supplies if dry conditions prevail.

GROUND WORKING

Hoe, weed, water and mulch all crops. Stake peas and runner beans.
Draw soil away from onions to hasten ripening.
Earth up potatoes.

FRUIT

PRUNING

Raspberries - Prune down old canes once new shoots are produced on newly planted canes. Select shoots and loosely tie-in.
Blackberries - Train in new shoots.
Gooseberries - Thin and summer prune at end of month.
Red/white currants - summer prune at end of month.
Cherries & plums - Continue to remove any fruits from fan-trained plants growing towards wall/fence. Pinch back other laterals and tie in.
Peaches/nectarines - Continue de-budding on wall trained plants and tie-in selected shoots. Thin fruits.
Plums - Thin in early June and finally late June.
Apples/Pears - If crop is heavy thin lightly and finally after June drop.
Figs - Pinch out top buds on young shoots at 5 leaves.

FERTILIZING

Apply nitrogen (light dressing) to strawberries if growth is poor. Commence foliar feeding with seaweed extract at least every two weeks.

PROTECTING

Continue to net soft fruits against birds if necessary.

WEEDING

Remove weeds from around all trees, bushes and canes.

WATERING

Set up irrigation system for summer use. Spray foliage in evening during hot weather.

GENERAL

Strawberries - straw down (or use black polythene or mats).
Ventilate protected plants.
Remove cloches and tunnels when fruiting has finished.
Peg down runners for new plants, otherwise remove them.
Carefully tie fragile new growths of all climbing (fruit) plants.

MONTHLY REMINDER

July MID-SUMMER

VEGETABLES

SOWING

OUTDOORS

Beetroot, cabbage (spring), calabrese, Oriental greens, texsel greens, chicory (sugar-loaf and red), endive, Florence fennel, kohlrabi, lettuce, parsley, peas (maincrop), radish (summer and winter), Swiss chard, turnips, salad plants.

FERTILIZING

Foliar feed all crops where necessary.

TRANSPLANTING

Sprouting broccoli, cabbage (winter), cauliflower (winter and spring heading), kale, leeks.

HARVESTING

GROUND

Globe artichokes, asparagus pea, French beans, runner beans, beetroot, cabbage (summer), calabrese, cauliflower (early summer), texsel greens, carrots, celery (self blanching), chicory (sugar-loaf), cucumber (outdoor), endive, Florence fennel, kohlrabi, lettuce, marrows, courgettes, squashes, pumpkins, onions (bulb and spring), parsley, peas, potatoes (early), radish (summer), rhubarb, spinach (New Zealand and summer), shallots, Swiss chard, sweetcorn, turnips, salad plants.

STORE

Garlic.

PROTECTING

Spray potatoes (maincrop) for blight. Check for pests and diseases - use organic control.

WATERING

Irrigate if necessary. Spray flowers of runner beans in the evening.

GROUND WORKING

Hoe, weed and mulch around all crops.

GENERAL

Tie-in and remove side shoots and tops of outdoor tomatoes after four or five trusses have formed. Earth up and stake brassicas on exposed sites. Hand pollinate marrows' and courgettes' female flowers if fruit is failing to set. Dry shallots ready for storing. Earth up celery.

FRUIT

PRUNING

Apples - complete thinning

Plums/cherries - continue training of fan shaped plants. Complete any pruning of cherry trees.

Blackberries - train new canes, undertake top layering for new plants.

Raspberries - immediately after fruiting cut out old canes and tie-in new ones. Remove unwanted suckers and control weeds.

Strawberries - immediately after summer-fruiting plants have fruited, cut off the old leaves and remove straw, remove surplus runners and all weeds, burn all debris.

FERTILIZING

Apply nitrogen (light dressing) to strawberries if growth is poor. Commence foliar feeding with seaweed extract at least every two weeks.

PROTECTING

Check trees for any constriction caused by ties and stakes.

Protect all fruits against birds.

WATERING

Set up irrigation system for summer use. Spray foliage in evening during hot weather.

HARVESTING

Strawberries, raspberries, gooseberries, blueberries, blackberries, loganberries, currants, cherries, peaches.

GENERAL

Support all heavily laden branches of trees. Ensure no broken branches, if any cut back cleanly. For plums protect surface with protective paint.

MONTHLY REMINDER

August LATE SUMMER

VEGETABLES

SOWING

OUTDOORS

Cabbage (spring) and Chinese cabbage, Oriental greens, texsel greens, chicory (sugar-loaf and red), endive, Florence fennel, Kohlrabi, lettuce (protected and outdoor winter), onions (bulb - autumn sown), spring onions (winter hardy), radish (summer and winter), scorzonera, Swiss chard, turnip, salad plants.

FERTILIZING

Foliar feed all crops where necessary.

TRANSPLANTING

UNPROTECTED - leeks.

PROTECTED - Florence fennel.

HARVESTING

GROUND

Globe artichokes, asparagus pea, aubergine, broad beans, French beans, runner beans, beetroot, cabbage (summer, autumn, Chinese), cauliflower (summer and early autumn), Oriental greens, texsel greens, carrots, celery (self-blanching), chicory (sugar-loaf and red), endive, Florence fennel, garlic, kohlrabi, lettuce, leeks, marrows, courgettes, squashes, pumpkins, onions (bulb and spring), parsley, potatoes (maincrop), radish (summer), spinach (New Zealand), shallots, Swiss chard, sweetcorn, tomatoes (outdoor), turnips, salad plants.

STORE

Garlic.

PROTECTING

Spray potatoes (maincrop) for blight. Check for pests and diseases - use organic control.

WATERING

Provide adequate amounts to beans, celery, celeriac, lettuce, peas (late sown).

GROUND WORKING

Hoe, weed and mulch around all crops.

GENERAL

Stop and stake outdoor tomatoes after 4/5 trusses set. Earth up and stake brassicas. Lift and dry onions. Cut off and burn potato hulm if affected by blight.

FRUIT

PLANTING

Prepare new strawberry beds and plant out rooted runners of summer fruiting varieties.

PRUNING

Plums, gages, damsons - carry out essential pruning after fruiting and cover large wounds with protective paint.

Apples and pears - continue pruning of restricted forms and over-vigorous trees.

Cobnuts and filberts - break laterals immediately after wall-trained peaches and nectarines have fruited, cut out the shoots which have borne fruit and dead wood and tie-in replacement shoots.

Fan-trained plums - remove dead wood, shorten pinched-back shoots and tie-in.

Raspberries - continue pruning and tying-in.

Blackberries - continue training new canes. Cut out old canes.

Raspberries, loganberries - cut out old canes.

PROTECTING

Continue to protect all fruits against birds.

WATERING

Set up irrigation system for summer use. Spray foliage in evening during hot weather.

HARVESTING

Apples (early varieties), pears, plums, peaches, apricots, blackberries, raspberries, loganberries, strawberries (perpetual).

GROUND WORKING

Prepare vacant ground for future planting digging deeply, work in compost or rotted manure. Remove all weeds.

GENERAL

Support heavily laden branches of all fruit trees.

September EARLY AUTUMN

MONTHLY REMINDER

VEGETABLES

SOWING

GREENHOUSE/FRAME/CLOCHE
Pak choi, chicory (sugar-loaf), radish (summer), salad plants.
Outdoors
Texsel greens, lettuce (protected and outdoor winter), radish (summer), spinach (winter), calabrese, salad plants.
Cauliflowers for transplanting to a frame in October.

PLANTING

Onions (sets - autumn plants).

FERTILIZING

Sow green manures on vacant plots.

TRANSPLANTING

UNPROTECTED
Cabbage (spring).
PROTECTED
Oriental greens, mizuna* and mustard*, Chinese cabbage, calabrese, komatsuna*, chicory (red and sugar-loaf), endive, Swiss chard, lettuces (*also survive outdoors in winter).

HARVESTING

GROUND
Aubergine, Runner beans, French beans, beetroot, Brussels sprouts, cabbage (autumn), calabrese, cauliflower (summer, early autumn and autumn), Oriental greens and texsel greens, carrots, celery (self-blanching), chicory (red and sugar-loaf), cucumber (outdoor), endive, Florence fennel, garlic, kohlrabi, leeks, lettuce, marrow, courgettes, squashes, pumpkin, onions (spring and bulb), parsley, parsnip, peas (maincrop), radish (summer), spinach (summer and New Zealand), Swiss chard, sweetcorn, tomatoes (outdoor), turnips, salad plants.
STORE
Onions lifted, dried off and stored. Potatoes lifted, dried and stored. Cut marrows and squashes (winter) for storage. Cut and ripen pumpkins.

GROUND WORKING

Make new compost heaps, apply compost to all vacant ground, sow green manures where required.

GENERAL

Start blanching cardoons. Earth-up celery - second time. Earth-up brassicas. Earth-up leeks (first time). Draw soil around celeriac roots. Clear spent crops, make compost with remains. Pull up tomato plants still bearing green fruits and hang up indoors or ripen under cloches.

FRUIT

PLANTING

Strawberries

PRUNING

Apples and pears - complete summer pruning.
Plums and damsons - prune immediately after collecting fruit.
Wall-trained peaches and nectarines - finish pruning.
Wall-trained cherries - remove dead wood. Tie down or cut out strong vertical shoots and complete typing-in.
Gooseberries - Complete pruning, cut off mildewed tops and burn.
Blackcurrants - Prune.
Blackberries - Cut off old canes after fruiting and tie in the new ones.

FERTILIZING

Apply nitrogen (light dressing) to strawberries if growth is poor. Commence foliar feeding with seaweed extract at least every two weeks.

PROTECTING

All fruits from birds and other animals, with netting.
Cover strawberries (perpetual) now fruiting with cloches towards end of month.
Continue spraying against apple and pear scab.

HARVESTING

Mid-season apples and pears, late plums and damsons, figs, grapes, raspberries (autumn fruiting), blackberries, blueberries, cobnuts and filberts.

MONTHLY REMINDER

October

MID-AUTUMN

VEGETABLES

SOWING

GREENHOUSE/FRAME/CLOCHE
Cauliflower (early summer), texsel greens, carrots, lettuce (winter), peas (early), radish (indoor), salads for seedling crops.

OUTDOOR
Broad beans, spinach (summer and winter).

PLANTING

Garlic, onions (sets).

TRANSPLANTING

UNPROTECTED — Cabbage (spring).

PROTECTED — Chinese broccoli, lettuce, Swiss chard.

HARVESTING

GROUND
Chinese artichoke, runner beans, French beans, beetroot, Brussels sprouts, cabbage and cauliflower (autumn), texsel greens, Oriental greens, carrots, celeriac, celery (self-blanching), chicory (red and sugar-loaf), endive, Florence fennel, kohlrabi, leeks, lettuce, onions (spring and bulb), parsley, parsnips, peas (maincrop), peppers, potatoes (maincrop), radish (summer), salsify, scorzonera, spinach (summer), swedes, Swiss chard, sweetcorn, tomatoes (outdoor), turnip, salad plants.

STORE
Garlic, potatoes (maincrop), shallots.

PROTECTING

Late cauliflowers from frost by covering curds. Cover parsley, herbs and salad plants with cloches.

GROUND WORKING

Dig and apply compost to bare plots. Apply lime if necessary. Make new compost heaps.

GENERAL

Lift and store beetroot, carrots, garlic, onions, potatoes (maincrop), shallots, winter chicory and cabbages, turnips.

Earth-up leeks, celery and celeriac.

Cut down asparagus fern, Jerusalem artichoke stems.

Clear away pea and bean supports.

Mulch rhubarb.

FRUIT

PLANTING

Trees, bushes, canes of top and soft fruit at end of month, depending upon soil conditions. Have fertilizers ready. Complete planting of strawberry runners.

PRUNING

Stone fruits - remove broken branches and protect the wounds.

Blackcurrants - prune if necessary.

Gooseberries, red and white currants - prune at leaf fall (if bird damage is likely pruning can be left until spring). Take cuttings.

Blackberries - finish pruning of hybrid berries.

PROTECTING

Cover strawberries with cloches to extend season.

Put grease bands around apple, pear and cherry trees.

Remove fallen leaves from around all apple and pear trees, to control scab.

HARVESTING

Strawberries, raspberries, blackberries, plums, apples and pears for storing.

STORING

Store fruit of sound condition. Bring down the temperature by ventilating at night. Do not mix late apples in the store with earlier cultivars, and keep apples and pears separate.

GENERAL

Tidy up strawberry beds and remove dead leaves from perpetuals. Order new fruit trees and bushes and start planting immediately after leaf fall. Prepare the ground for planting before the trees arrive.

MONTHLY REMINDER

November EARLY AUTUMN

VEGETABLES

SOWING

GREENHOUSE/FRAME/CLOCHE
Peas (early).

OUTDOOR
Broad beans, spring cabbage.

PLANTING

Garlic, onions (sets), rhubarb.

HARVESTING

GROUND
Jerusalem and Chinese artichoke, Brussels sprouts, cabbage (winter), cauliflower (autumn), Oriental greens, carrots, celeriac, chicory (red and sugar-loaf), endive, kohlrabi, leeks, lettuce (protected winter), parsley, spinach (summer and winter), swedes, Swiss chard, turnips, salad plants.

STORE
Beetroot, carrots, garlic, onions (bulb), potatoes (maincrop), shallots. Check stored vegetables for signs of rotting.

FORCING

Chicory, seakale.

PROTECTING

Lift and store beetroot, carrots, turnips, swede. Protect celeriac and globe artichokes with bracken. Cover with straw root crops overwintered in the ground. Heel cauliflowers over to protect from frost.

GROUND WORKING

Carry on with digging and manuring when conditions are favourable. Clean up fallen leaves and put in heap to make leaf mould. Make new compost heaps.

GENERAL

Remove yellow and decaying leaves from stems of Brussels sprouts and other brassicas. Cloche perpetual spinach and cover endive with flower pots to blanch it. Cover the completed compost heap with polythene sheeting or other waterproof material. Cut down any dead asparagus 'fern' and cover the bed or rows with compost or rotted manure.

FRUIT

PLANTING

All top and soft fruits can be planted from now until early spring. This is the ideal month because the ground is still warm, but it is better to postpone planting than to attempt it in very unfavourable conditions.

PRUNING

Apples and pears - on summer pruned trees prune back to mature wood where secondary shoots have been produced. Prune established trees immediately after leaf fall. Carry on the formative pruning of dwarf pyramid, espalier and fan forms. Young tip-bearing cordons or those lacking vigour can be tipped.

Blackberries - complete pruning.

Raspberries - complete pruning.

Check supports and wires and ensure canes are securely tied.
Currants and gooseberries - prune.

PROTECTING

Ensure fruit cage is closed and the netting is in good order. Loosely bundle fig branches together and cover with mats or straw to provide winter protection. Mulch the rooting areas with straw or bracken. Loosely bundle the new canes of blackberries together and tie to a wire for winter protection.

HARVESTING

Finish picking all but the very late apples and pears.

GENERAL

Root prune over-vigorous trees after leaf fall.

VEGETABLES

SOWING

GREENHOUSE/FRAME/CLOCHE
Rhubarb, shallots.

OUTDOOR
Broad beans.

TRANSPLANTING

PROTECTED
Lettuce - sown in October.

HARVESTING

GROUND
Chinese and Jerusalem artichoke, Brussels sprouts, cabbage (winter), cauliflower (winter heading), Oriental greens, carrots, celeriac, chicories, endive, kohl rabi, leeks, lettuce (protected winter), parsley, parsnips, radishes, salsify, scorzonera, spinach (winter), swede, Swiss chard, turnip, salad plants.

STORE
Beetroot, carrots, garlic, onions (bulb), potatoes (maincrop), shallots, marrow. Check stored vegetables for signs of rotting.

FORCING

Chicory (witloof), rhubarb, seakale.

PROTECTING

Protect globe artichokes with straw or better still, with dry pulverized bark and cloches. Protect the exposed tops of celery with straw.

GROUND WORKING

Clear away debris, continue digging and composting if weather conditions permit.

GENERAL

Lift and store carrots and swede. Make list of varieties that have done well. Apply crop rotation plan.

FRUIT

PLANTING

Plant all fruits when soil conditions are suitable. If the soil is too wet, loosen the bundles, remove the packing material and heel the plants in. If the soil is frozen keep the plants in a cool, frost-proof place. Ensure roots do not dry out and plant as soon as possible.

PRUNING

Apples, pears, bush and cane fruits - continue pruning except in hard freezing conditions, dealing with the young trees first, and then the older trees. Collect the prunings and burn.

PROTECTING

Check the condition of all stakes, supports and ties for trees.

Check grease bands.

Look for and remedy wind rocking or constriction.

Tie fig shoots together and cover with straw and sacking.

Remove any unwanted fruit from trees.

SPRAYING

Start spraying of dormant trees, bush and cane fruits with winter wash to control aphids, sucker and scale insects.

Complete the spraying of stone fruits by the end of the month. Inspect the apples and pears for canker and treat where necessary.

HARVESTING

Complete picking of very late apples before hard frosts appear.

GENERAL

Erect a polythene cover over fan-trained peaches and nectarines against peach leaf curl.

Inspect stored fruits and remove rotten ones.

CONCLUSION

GLOSSARY

Abiotic Non-living parts of the ecosystem, such as climate and physical components of soil or the landscape.

Absorption The process by which a substance is taken into and included within another substance.

Acid Soil with little or no lime content, having a pH level of 6.5 or less. Over acidity is harmful to plant growth and is remedied by the addition of some form of lime. It occurs mostly on peat soils, on some sandy soils and in areas of high rainfall.

Activator Anything used in a compost heap to hasten the conversion of vegetable waste into usable compost. It may be a proprietary compound, seaweed or small quantities of animal manure placed between layers of other material.

Aerobic Requiring free oxygen, or relating to a condition in which free oxygen is present.

Alkaline soil Soil with a high lime content, having a pH value of more than 7.4.

Alleopathy The process whereby a plant restricts the growth or development of other plants around it by releasing toxic chemicals.

Alternative hosts Also referred to as decoy plants, these are plants that are used to attract insect pests away from the principal crop.

Anaerobic Not requiring free oxygen or relating to a condition in which free oxygen is not present.

Annual Plant that grows from seed and completes its lifecycle in less than 12 months.

Base dressing Fertilizer worked into the soil prior to sowing or planting.

Beneficial insects Those insects that are helpful to the gardener because they pollinate plants or prey on pests.

Biennial Plant whose lifecycle spans two years. The seed germinates and grows into a leafy tuft or rosette the first year, then the plant flowers, seeds and dies in the following year.

Blanch To exclude light from plants to render them white and tender.

Blight A disease characterized by sudden leaf, flower, or stem death.

Bolt To flower prematurely, usually owing to unsuitable growing conditions or the effect of day length.

Broadcast To sow by scattering seed thinly over a prepared site and raking it in, instead of sowing in a drill.

Calcifuge A plant that dislikes alkaline soil.

Canker A diseased or dying area on a stem, branch or twig.

Cap Soil is said to be capped when heavy rain or watering causes the surface to run together and form a hard crust when dry, a condition seriously affecting seedlings and germinating seeds. The cap should be broken up as close to the row as possible by very careful hoeing.

Catch crop Crop sown on temporarily vacant ground intended for another. The catch crop must be quick-maturing and may overlap the main crop by a few weeks if necessary.

Cation A positively charged ion. The basic nutrient cations of calcium, potassium and magnesium and the acidic cations of aluminium and hydrogen account for nearly all the adsorbed cations in the soil. Micronutrient cations include iron, manganese and zinc. Nitrogen may be present, either as a cation (ammonium), or as an anion (nitrate) in the soil solution.

Cation exchange capacity (CEC) An important measure of the soil's ability to retain and to supply nutrients to plants. The bulk of this capacity resides in soil organic matter and clay particles. CEC is important because it represents the primary soil reservoir of readily available potassium, calcium and magnesium and several micronutrients. It also helps prevent their leaching.

Check Growth halted through adverse conditions such as drought, cold, starvation or delayed planting.

Chlorophyll The green pigment found in plants' leaves and stems.

Chlorosis Yellowing of normally green tissue caused by destruction of chlorophyll or failure of its formation.

Clamp Method of storing root crops, to protect them from frost, in which the roots are piled on a base of straw, then covered with straw and earth, either outdoors or inside a shed.

Clone A group of identical plants that have been vegetatively propagated from the same source.

Companion plants Plants that relate in a positive way to their neighbouring plants.

Compost Waste vegetable matter decomposed in heaps or containers to a point at which the plant foods in it become available when dug into the soil.

Composts, seeds and potting An entirely different meaning of the word, referring to the special soils for sowing seeds and growing plants in pots and other containers.

Cordon Plant growing up a single stem.

Cover Term used to describe any form of protection for plants, such as a greenhouse, frame, cloche or a windowsill indoors.

Cover crops Crops that are planted to protect the ground between the harvest of one main crop and the sowing of the next. These crops protect soil from erosion as well as build soil organic matter and control weeds.

Crown Term used to describe the top of the root system of a perennial plant, or sometimes the whole root system.

Cultivar A variety of a plant originating in cultivation as opposed to in the wild.

Curd The white head of the cauliflower. The curd of the winter cauliflower is protected from frost by a close ring of leaves. Curds of summer cauliflowers should be sheltered from the sun by bending outer leaves over them.

Cutting A piece of stem cut away from a plant to be rooted in order to produce a new plant.

Damping off Destruction of seedlings at the soil line, which can be caused by many pathogens.

Dioecious Having male and female flowers on separate plants. Both male and female plants are required for pollination.

Division Method of propagation in which the plant is split into several parts so that each part can grow into a separate new plant.

Dormant period Natural resting stage in the annual cycle of a plant's growth - literally 'sleeping'. The time when a plant is not in active growth. Particularly the time from autumn to spring.

Double digging Breaking up the soil to the depth of two spades.

Drill Small trench in which seeds are sown. Drills are usually made with a draw hoe and vary in depth and width with the size of the seed and the season of the year.

Earthing up The drawing up of earth around the base and stem of a plant. It may be done to blanch the stems in the case of celery, or to prevent greening of the tubers by light in the case of potatoes.

Evergreen A plant that does not lose its leaves but has them all year round.

F1 hybrid A variety produced by the crossing of 2 distinct parent strains. These hybrids are noted for their vigour and productivity. An F1 hybrid cannot be reproduced from its own seed.

Farmyard manure Manure produced by cattle, horses, chickens, etc. For safe use in the garden it must be well-rotted or composted thoroughly.

Fertilizer Inorganic plant food. A straight fertilizer contains only one of the three principal elements essential to the plant, a compound, general or balanced fertilizer contains all three.

Forcing Bringing a plant into earlier growth, generally by raising the temperature under which it is grown.

Friable soil Soil that is crumbly in texture.

Frost hollow A low-lying area subject to spring frosts. In any garden laid out on a slope it should be remembered that fruit blossom will be less liable to damage on the higher part as cold air flows downwards and collects at the lowest point.

Fungus An undifferentiated plant that lacks chlorophyll and conductive tissue. Examples include moulds, rusts, smuts, rots and mushrooms.

Genus (plural genera) Category of plant classification by grouping plants having similar characteristics. It is subdivided into species and is represented by the first element in a botanical name.

Germination The first stage in the development and growth of a seed.

Glaucous Covered in a bluish bloom.

Good heart Vague but often-used expression denoting soil fertility. It implies that the soil has been well manured in the past, is well cultivated and not weed-infested.

Green manure The practice of growing crops which are later dug into the soil either as a source of humus or a source of minerals, depending on the crop used.

Ground cover Plants grown to cover large areas of soil in the garden. They are often planted to keep weeds down and prevent soil erosion.

Growing days The number of days in a year between the point when average daytime temperatures reach about 6°C/43°F in spring, and fall back to that point in winter. Most plants cease to grow below that temperature.

Growing on Stage in the production of a plant under glass following pricking out.

Hardening off The process of gradually acclimatizing a plant that has been raised indoors to lower temperatures, so that it is not severely checked when it is planted outside. It is done by standing the plants in the open and bringing them in or covering with cloches at night for a week or so, or by putting them in a frame and leaving the light off for increasing periods.

Hardy/ half hardy Term used of plants in the temperate zone that live outside from year to year without any kind of protection. Generally taken to mean a plant which can be exposed to frost. Half-hardy plants can survive only limited cold and need a sheltered or protected site, or removal to a more or less frost-free place for winter.

Haulm The stems and vines of certain crops such as potatoes, peas and runner beans.

Herbicides Chemicals used to kill off vegetation, in particular weeds.

Hosts Plants that attract insects because they are a good source of nectar, pollen or other food.

Humus The organic content of soil, formed by the breakdown of organic matter and essential to fertility. It is usually dark in colour.

Hybrid A plant created by crossing two dissimilar parent plants.

Inoculant A material of high microbial content that is added to soil or compost to stimulate biological activity.

Insecticides Chemicals used to combat insect pests.

In situ Used for seed sown where the plant is to grow, to avoid transplanting.

Intercropping Growing two or more crops together to make the best use of the ground available or because of the mutual benefit they afford each other. Also known as interplanting.

Lateral A side shoot or branch, springing from a main stem or larger branch. The cutting back of laterals is an important part of fruit tree pruning and in the growing of tall varieties of tomatoes no laterals are allowed to develop, being rubbed out as soon as they are seen.

Larva An immature form of an insect that differs radically from the adult form.

Leaching Use of soluble fertilizers and such substances as lime that are washed deep into the soil out of reach of plant roots, or out of the bottom of containers by rain or continual watering.

Leader The main shoot of a stem or branch, with the growing point at its tip.

Leafmold Partially decayed leaves, useful for incorporating into the soil as humus.

Legume / Leguminous plants Plants belonging to the pea family. They are important in crop rotation leaving the soil richer in nitrogen if their roots are left to decay. This is because the roots carry nodules containing colonies of bacteria which fix atmospheric nitrogen. Peas, beans, clovers and vetches are examples of leguminous crops.

Lesion A spot or area of diseased tissue.

Loam Ideal soil type in which particles of clay, silt, sand and organic matter are well balanced and blended.

Maggot The larva of a fly.

Micro-climate The climate of a very localized area, such as a garden or part of a garden, or even the immediate surroundings of a plant.

Micronutrient A plant nutrient needed in very small amounts, including copper, zinc, iron, manganese, boron, and molybdenum. Also called trace elements.

Mineralization The conversion of an organic form of an element to the inorganic state, generally through microbial decomposition. Mineralization allows plants to absorb soil nutrients through their roots.

Monocrops Crops of a single variety filling the whole of the garden or plot.

Mosaic A symptom of certain viral diseases characterized by mottled, intermingled patterns of yellow and green on the leaves.

Mulch A cover or a protective material, anything from polythene film to manure, placed around the plant primarily to help retain moisture in the soil and to restrict the growth of weeds.

Mycorrhiza A symbiotic association of a fungus with the roots of a plant.

Nematode Non-segmented, microscopic wormlike animals that live in soil, water, plants, animals, and dead organic matter.

Neutral soil Soil that is neither acid not alkaline having a pH of 7.0.

Open An open soil is one naturally loose and friable, like a sandy loam or a heavier soil generously manured; such soils permit good root development. Open weather refers to any period in winter when there is hard frost or heavy rain.

Organic As an agricultural term, it usually refers to a method of farming or gardening without the use of synthetic pesticides or fertilizers. In organic gardening only such materials, compost, animal manures, or such products as fish meal and bone meal, are used as plant foods. As a general biological term, it refers to something derived from plants and animals. As a term used by chemists, it refers to compounds of carbon other than inorganic carbonates.

Organic matter The fraction of the soil that includes plant and animal remains, residues, or their waste products in various stages of decomposition. Anything that is, or has been living matter.

Parasites An organism that lives and feeds on another organism for at least part of its life cycle. Usually, only one host organism is required for the complete development of the parasite. Plants that grow on other plants on which they are dependent for food and support.

Pathogen An organism capable of causing disease in other organisms.

Pest Any organism (weed, disease, insect, mite, vertebrate, etc) that interferes with human activity or causes injury, loss or irritation to a crop, stored product, an animal or people.

Pesticide A substance used to kill pests.

pH soil A measure of the concentration of hydrogen ions in the soil solution and a primary factor in optimum plant growth. When pH is maintained at the optimal level for a given crop, plant nutrients are at maximum availability and toxic elements are at reduced availability. On a scale of 1 to 14, a pH of 7.0 is neutral, lower numbers indicate acidity, and higher numbers indicate alkalinity.

Pheromone A chemical substance (such as a sexual attractant) secreted by an insect that influences the behaviour of other individuals of the same species.

Plant association The way plants relate to other plants.

Pollination The fertilization of a flower by the transfer of pollen from male to female parts to produce seed or fruit. Some varieties of fruit are self-sterile and cannot be fertilized by their own pollen, so requiring a tree of another variety, blooming at the same time, to act as a pollinator.

Pot-bound Condition in which a plant's root system has outgrown the pot in which it is planted, shown by the soil ball being enclosed in a dense mass of root. Plants such as tomatoes and marrows, intended for outdoor planting, should not be allowed to become pot-bound, as they are liable to be starved and badly checked. It is unwise to start such crops too early under glass if they cannot be planted out for fear of frost.

Predators Animals or Insects that eat other animals or insects. A predator usually needs to feed on more than one host to complete its development.

Pricking out Transferring seedlings from seed tray to pots or other containers where they have more room. It should be done as early as possible, preferably before the seedlings get their first true leaves. The longer it is left, the more entangled they become, the greater the damage done to their roots, and the longer they take to recover.

Propagation The means of increasing the numbers of a plant.

Prostrate Close to the ground, low growing.

Pupa An inactive stage of an insect, between larva and adult, in which adult features develop.

Resistance The ability of an organism to remain relatively healthy despite infection by a pathogen.

Rhizobia Nitrogen-fixing bacteria that live in symbiosis with legumes.

Rhizome An elongated underground stem, usually horizontal, capable of producing new shoots and roots at the nodes.

Rhizosphere The soil around living plant roots.

Ring culture Method of growing tomatoes under glass. The tomato is planted in potting compost in a cylindrical pot open at both ends ('tompot') standing on a bed of shingle or clinker. This is kept watered and the tomato roots into it, liquid feeds being applied only to the compost. The method reduces the frequency of watering compared to ordinary pot culture and is very useful in a greenhouse which has to be left unattended during the day.

Rootstock The root on to which a fruit tree is grafted. It is the main influence in deciding the size of the tree at maturity and the quickness with which it comes into bearing.

Rotation of crops The yearly movement of crops from one place in the garden to another to make the best use of the ground and to reduce the incidence of pests and diseases. A plan of rotation cannot be followed exactly, but continuously growing the same crops on the same ground is a sure recipe for trouble.

Saprophyte An organism that feeds on dead organic matter.

Seed-leaf The first leaf to appear from the seed on germination, usually different in form from those that follow, known as true leaves. If the seed-leaf is damaged, as by attacks of flea beetle, the seedling is crippled and may not survive.

Set State of a flower which will form fruit after successful pollination.

Soft fruit Fruit produced on bushes, canes or plants, as opposed to top fruit, produced on trees. Soft fruit gives the quicker return on investment and the best opportunities for fruit production in the small garden.

Soil ball Compact mass of potting compost and roots of a pot-grown plant. The soil ball should be disturbed as little as possible when planting out.

Soil erosion The washing or blowing away of soil by winds, rains and floods.

Soil mulch It is a layer of loose soil produced by regular hoeing in dry weather. This prevents soil moisture being drawn to the surface by capillary action.

Soil sickness A disease caused by repeatedly growing the same crop in the same soil.

Soil structure The physical arrangement of soil particles. A good soil structure contains aggregates (connected units of minerals and organic material) of widely varying size, with adequate "pore space" between soil particles to allow ready movement of water, air, and other soil nutrients.

Species An individual or closely related group of plants within a genus.

Spore The reproductive unit of fungi, analogous to the seed of green plants. Resting structures of some bacteria also are called spores.

Spur Short lateral growth on a fruit tree, described as a fruiting spur if it bears one or more fruit buds. The main aim in pruning mature trees is to encourage the production of fruiting spurs.

Stop To pinch out the growing point of a main stem or lateral.

Subsoil Soil layer immediately below the normal depth of digging. It may be of clay, gravel or chalk and determines the nature of the topsoil above it. Because no organic matter has accumulated in the subsoil, it is relatively infertile except as a source of minerals, and must be kept separate from the fertile layer above it.

Successional cropping The planting of a new crop as soon as one is harvested so that the ground is always in use.

Successional planting The positioning of plants in a garden so that one takes its place visually as the other dies back.

Successional sowing Sowing of a quick-maturing crop to make use of ground previously occupied by a main crop, such as stump-rooted carrots following early potatoes and being pulled in October. Also, frequent small sowings of crops such as lettuce and radish which deteriorate quickly and of which a continuous supply is needed.

Sucker A shoot other than the main stem that produces a new plant when it grows to the soil surface. Globe artichokes are propagated by planting sucker growths in spring and raspberries by planting suckers in autumn.

Synthetic Produced artificially, or man-made, rather than occurring naturally.

Tender Plants unable to withstand frosts.

Texture The relative proportions of sand, silt and clay in a particular soil.

Thinning The process of reducing the number of seedlings in a row so that the remaining ones have room to grow.

Tilth The physical condition of the surface of the soil. A fine tilth is required for sowing seeds, larger ones like beans tolerate a slightly more lumpy seed bed. On heavy soils the best tilth is obtained by leaving the soil in clods exposed to winter frosts. If this opportunity is missed, it is rarely possible to 'force a tilth' by any amount of mechanical action such as raking.

Tolerant Capable of sustaining an infection by a pathogen or of enduring environmental stress or injury without much damage.

Vegetative propagation/ reproduction Propagation by methods other than seed. Treating part of a plant in such a way that it becomes a separate plant, producing a plant identical to its parent. Top fruits are propagated by grafting a stem of the variety being united to a special rootstock.

Variety Plant produced by selective breeding and hybridization and having characteristics which distinguish it from other varieties of the same species.

Waterlogging A waterlogged soil is not merely wet, it is full of water unable to drain away. Normally, air is sucked into the soil as the water drains out, but this is impossible in waterlogged conditions and plant roots die for lack of oxygen.

BIBLIOGRAPHY

GENERAL

Vegetables
Roger Phillips & Martin Rix
Macmillan 1995

Month by Month Organic Gardening
Lawrence D Hills
Thorsons 1983

Food from your Garden
Readers Digest 1997

Encyclopaedia of Gardening
Christopher Brickell
Dorling Kindersley 1992

Enchanted Garden
Tom Cuthbertson
Rider & Co/Hutchinson 1979

Soil Humus of Health
Dr W.E. Sherwell-Cooper
Good Gardeners Assn. 1993

Composting: The Natural Organic Way
Dick Kitto
Thorsons 1988

Home Grown
Keith Mossman & Mary Norwak
Spectator Publications 1977

Down to Earth Fruit & Vegetable Growing
Lawrence D Hills
Faber & Faber 1960

The Fruit Garden Displayed
Harry Baker
The Royal Horticultural Society 1991

The Ornamental Kitchen Garden
Janet Macdonald
David & Charles 1994

Creative Vegetable Gardening
Joy Larkcom
Mitchell Beazley/Edenlite 1997

The Complete Fruit Book
Bob Flowerdew
Kyle Cathie Ltd 1995

The Complete Book of Self-Sufficiency
John Seymour
Faber 1976

The New Organic Gardener
Eliot Coleman
Cassell 1989

Four Season Harvest
Eliot Coleman
Chelsea Green 1992

Designing and Maintaining Your Edible Landscape Naturally
Robert Kourik
Metamorphic Press 1986

How to Grow More Vegetables
John Jeavons
Ten Speed Press 1982

Unusual Vegetables
Anne Moyer Halpin
Rodale Press 1978

The Gaia Book of Organic Gardening
Patrick Holden
Gaia Books 2005

Practical Allotment Gardening
Caroline Foley
New Holland 2002

The Allotment Handbook
Caroline Foley
New Holland 2004

Kitchen Garden
Andi Clevely
Harper Collins 1999

Pippa's Organic Kitchen Garden
Pippa Greenwood
Dorling Kindersley 1999

COMPANION PLANTING

A-Z Companion Planting
Pamela Allardice
Cassell 1993

The Companion Gardener
Bob Flowerdew
Kyle Cathie Ltd 1991

Complete Book of Companion Gardening
Bob Flowerdew
Kyle Cathie Ltd 1993

Companion Planting
Gertrude Franck
Thorsons 1983

Forest Gardening
Robert Hart
Green Broods 1991

Introduction to Permaculture
Bill Mollison
Tagari Publications 1991

Bio-Dynamic Gardening
John Soper
Bio-Dynamic Assn. USA 1983

Companion Planting in Australia
Brenda Little
Reed

Companion Plants
Helen Phillrick & Richard Gregg
Broadcast Books 1991

Carrots Love Tomatoes
V.T. Pownal
Garden Way Publishing USA 1984

Primer of Companion Planting
Richard Gregg
Bio-Dynamic Assn, USA

GARDENING BY THE MOON

Work on the Land and the Constellations
Maria Thun
The Landthorn Press

"Stella Natura"
Biodynamic Agricultural Centre, Kimberton PA 19442 USA
(Published annually)

'The Art of Timing'
(The Application of Lunar Cycles in Daily Life)
Johanna Paungger & Thomas Pope
The CurDaniel Co Ltd, 2000

How to Grow More Vegetables
John Jeavors
Ten Speed Press USA 1992

Enchanted Garden
Tom Cuthbertson,
Rider & Co/Hutchinson,
London 1979

Planting by the Moon
Geraldine Murfin-Shaw
154 Regent Street, Nelson,
Lancs BB9 8SG
£8.50 inc p & p

ACKNOWLEDGEMENTS

Many thanks must go to the following people for without their kind assistance, this book would not have been possible.

Manuscript Comments

Gaby Bartai-Bevan	Writer and Editor, *Organic Gardening*	Shetland
Lin Hawthorne	Head Gardener	Yorkshire
Mike Hedges	Director Chase Organics	Surrey
Fiona Hopes	Garden Designer and Author	Worcestershire
Noel Kingsbury	Writer and Author	Herefordshire
Mick Lavelle	Senior Lecturer in Landscape Management, Writtle College	Essex
Elspeth Thompson	Writer and Author	London

Graphic Design

Andrew Crane	Graphic Designer and Artist	Somerset

Secretarial

Ruth Arnold	Secretary	Somerset
Mary Coles	Secretary and PA	Somerset

CREDITS

Richard Bird
Companion Planting
© Quarto Publishing Ltd
- Plant Distress Signals
- Pest Deterrents
- Hosts & Insects
- Sprays & Oils

Peter Harper
The Natural Garden Book
© Gaia Books Ltd a division of the Octopus Publishing Group 1994
- Soil Additives
- Dynamic Accumulators
- Mineral Deficiency Signs
- Weed Management
- Bio-Dynamic Preparations
- Pest Controls

George Seddon
Your Kitchen Garden
© Mitchell Beazley Ltd
- Two Illustrations
- Average Temperatures & Phenological Map

Michael Lavelle
Organic Gardening
© Anness Publishing Ltd
- Plant Nutrient Guide
- Greenhouse Cropping Plan
- Illustration – A Typical Garden and its Microclimate
- Nutrient Cycles in a Typical Garden

Pauline Pears
Encyclopedia of Organic Gardening
© Dorling Kindersley Penguin Group.
- Soil Structure Indicators
- Biological Control Plants
- Permitted Pesticides
- Ingredients Suitable for Growing Media
- Plant Raising & Potting Mixes

Adams & Pearly
Principles of Horticulture
© Elsevior
- Carbon and Nitrogen Cycles

L & G.V. Poisson
Solar Gardening
© Chelsea Green Publishing Co
- Succession Planting
- Organic Matter Plant Products
- Organic Matter
- Animal Manures
- Organic Matter
- Animal By-products
- Green Manures
- Minerals
- Organic Fertilizers

Bob Flowerdew
Go Organic
© Hamlyn — a division of Octopus Publishing Group
- Organic Pesticides
- Biological Controls

Jekka McVicar
Complete Book of Vegetables
Herbs & Fruits
© Kyle Cathie Ltd
- A Note on Botanical Names

Jennifer Davies
The Wartime Kitchen & Garden
published by BBC Books/Random House Ltd
- Illustration Cropping Plan
- Extract from Ministry Dig for Victory Campaign

Alan Titchmarsh
Gardening Under Cover
© Hamlyn, a division of Octopus Publishing Group
- Greenhouse, Frame & Cloche Cropping Plans

John Jeavons
How To Grow More Vegetables
published by Ten Speed Press USA

ORGANIC ORGANIZATIONS

UK

Garden Organic
Ryton Organic Gardens
Coventry CV8 3LG
Tel: 02476-303517
Email: enquiry@hydra.org.uk
www.hydra.org.uk

Plants for a Future
The Field
Higher Penpol, Lostwithiel
Cornwall PL22 0NG
Email: pfaf@scs.leeds.ac.uk
www.scs.leeds.ac.uk/pfaf

Royal Society for the Protection of Birds
The Lodge
Sandy
Bedfordshire SG19 2DI
www.rspb.org.uk

Soil Association
Bristol House, 40-56 Victoria Street
Bristol BS1 6BY
Tel: 0117-929-0661
Email: info@soilassociation.org
www.soilassociation.org

The Wildlife Trusts UK Office
The Kiln, Waterside, Mather Road
Newark NG24 1WT
Tel: 01636 677711
www.wildlifetrusts.org

Bio-Dynamic Agriculture Association
Painswick Inn Project
Gloucester Street
Stroud
Glos GL5 1Q
Tel: 01453 759501
Fax: 01453 759501
E: bdaa@biodynamic.freeserve.co.uk

Centre for Alternative Technology
Machynlleth
Powys SY20 9AZ
Tel: 01654 705950
Fax: 01654 702782
www.cat.org.uk

USA

The Rodale Institute
611 Siegfriedale Road
Kutztown, PA 19530-9320
Tel: (610) 683-1400
www.rodaleinstitute.org

CANADA

The National Information Network for Organic Farmers, Gardeners & Consumers
Box 6408, Station J
Tel: (613) 767-0796
Ottawa, Ontario K2A 3Y6
www.cog.ca

Nanaimo Community Gardens Society
271 Pine Street
Nanaimo
British Columbia V9R 2B7
www.communitygardens.tripod.com/nanaimo

Nova Scotia Organic Growers Association
3101 Highway, 236, RR #1
Kennetcook, Nova Scotia B0N 1P0
www.gks.com/NSOGA

AUSTRALIA

Organic Federation of Australia Inc
PO Box Q455
QVB Post Office
Sydney NSW 1230
Tel: (61) 2 9299 8016
Fax: (61) 2 9299 0189
Email: info@ofa.org.au

ORGANIC SUPPLIERS

Chase Organics
River Dene Estate
Molesey Road, Hersham
Surrey KT12 4RG
Tel: 01932 243666
Fax: 01932 252707

Chilterns Seeds
Bortree Stile, Ulverston
Cumbria LA12 7PB
Tel: 01229 581137
Fax: 01229 584549

Future Foods
PO Box 1564, Wedmore
Somerset BS28 4DP
Tel: 01934 713623
Fax: 01934 713623

Heritage Seed Library
c/o Garden Organic
Ryton Organic Gardens
Coventry CV8 3LG
Tel: 02476 303517

Mr Fothergill's Seeds
Gazeley Road
Kentford, Newmarket
Suffolk CB8 7QB
Tel: 01638 751161
Fax: 01638 751624

Suffolk Herbs
Monks Farm, Coggleshall Road
Kelvedon
Essex CO5 9PG
Tel: 01376 572456
Fax: 01376 571189

Pinetum Products
Pinetum Lodge
Churcham
Glos GL2 8AD
Tel: 07901 815647

Tamar Organics
The Organic Garden Centre
Tavistock Woodlands Estate
Gulworthy
Devon PL19 8JE

Thompson and Morgan
Poplar Lane, Ipswich
Suffolk IP8 3BU
Tel: 01473 688821
Fax: 01473 680199

ORGANIC GARDENING MAGAZINES

ORGANIC GARDENING
Monthly

THE ORGANIC WAY
Quarterly

ORGANIC LIFE
Monthly

LIVING EARTH
Quarterly

PERMACULTURE
Monthly

CONVERSION TABLES

	Metric	Imperial
LENGTH	1 millimetre (mm)	0.0394 in
	1 centimetre (cm)/10mm	0.3937 in
	1 metre/100cm	39.37 in/3.281 ft/1.094 yd
	1 kilometre (km) 1000 metres	1093.6 yd/0.6214 mile
	25.4mm/2.54cm	1 inch
	304.8mm/30.48cm/0.3048m	1 foot (ft) 12in
	914.4mm/91.44cm/0.9144m	1 yard (yd) 3ft
	1609.344 metres/1.609km	1 mile/1760 yd
AREA	1 square centimetre(sq cm)/ 100 sq millimetres(sq mm)	0.155 sq in
	1 square metre(sq m)/10,000sq cm	10.764 sq ft/1.196 sq yd
	1 are/100 sq metres	119.60 sq yd/0.0247 acre
	1 hectare (ha)/100 ares	2.471 acres/0.00386 sq mile
	645.16 sq mm/6.4516 sq cm	1 square inch(sq in)
	929.03 sq cm	1 square foot(sq ft) 144sq in
	8361.3 sq cm/0.8361 sq m	1 square yard(sq yd)/9 sq ft
	4046.9 sq m/0.4047 ha	1 acre/4840 sq yd
	259 ha/2.59 sq km	1 square mile/640 acres
VOLUME	1 cubic centimetre (cu cm)/ 10000 cubic millimetres (cu mm)	0.0610 cu in
	1 cubic decimetre (cu dm)/1000 cu cm	61.024 cu in/0.0353 cu ft
	1 cubic metre/1000 cu dm	35.3147 cu ft/1.308 cu yd
	1 cu cm = 1 millilitre (ml)	
	1 cu dm = 1 litre (see Capacity)	
	16.3871 cu cm	1 cubic inch (cu in)
	28,316.8 cu cm/0.0283 cu metre	1 cubic foot (cu ft)/1728 cu in
	0.7646 cu metre	1 cubic yard (cu yd)/27 cu ft
CAPACITY	1 litre	1.7598 pt/0.8799 qt/0.22 gal
	0.568 litre	1 pint (pt)
	1.137 litres	1 quart (qt)
	4.546 litres	1 gallon (gal)
	1 gram(g)	0.035 oz
	1 kilogram (kg)/1000 g	2.20 lb/35.2 oz
	1 tonne/1000 kg	2204.6 lb/0.9842 ton
WEIGHT	28.35 g	1 ounce (oz)
	0.4536 kg	1 pound (lb)
	1016 kg	1 ton
	1 gram per square metre (g/metre²)	0.0295 oz/sq yd
	1 gram per square centimetre (g/cm²)	0.228 oz/sq in
	1 kilogram per square centimetre (kg/cm²)	14.223 lb/sq in
	1 kilogram per square metre (kg/metre²)	0.205 lb/sq ft
TEMPERATURE	To convert °F to °C, subtract 32, then divide by 9 and multiply by 5 To convert °C to °F, divide by 5 and multiply by 9, then add 32	

INDEX

R

S

T

V

W

Y

Z